OUTSPOKEN

OUTSPOKEN

50 SPEECHES
BY INCREDIBLE
WOMEN

From
**Boudicca to
Michelle Obama**

DEBORAH COUGHLIN

1 3 5 7 9 10 8 6 4 2

WH Allen, an imprint of Ebury Publishing
20 Vauxhall Bridge Road,
London SW1V 2SA

WH Allen is part of the Penguin Random House group of companies
whose addresses can be found at global.penguinrandomhouse.com

Penguin
Random House
UK

First published by WH Allen in 2019
This edition published by WH Allen in 2019

www.penguin.co.uk

A CIP catalogue record for this book is available from the British Library

ISBN 9780753554050

Printed and bound in Great Britain by Clays Ltd, Elcograf S.p.A.

Penguin Random House is committed to a sustainable future for our
business, our readers and our planet. This book is made from Forest
Stewardship Council® certified paper.

This book is for the fifth wave …

Alex, Bobby, Dan, Florence, Idahlia, Iris, Toby,

Ruby and the Ariana Grande brunch crew

1. The best boys love feminism.
2. Don't be persuaded that we no longer need feminism until the last woman is liberated.

Contents

CHAPTER 10

WHY OUTSPOKEN?

' … you don't have the alibi my class had – this is one of the great achievements and mixed blessings you inherit: Unlike us, you can't say nobody told you there were other options. Twenty-five years from now, you won't have as easy a time making excuses as my class did. You won't be able to blame the deans, or the culture, or anyone else: you will have no one to blame but yourselves. Whoa!'
Nora Ephron, Filmmaker and Writer, addressing the graduates of Wellesley College, USA, in 1996

Imagine if every time we humans invented something we then forgot how that invention works.

For instance, if we all got collective amnesia and forgot how light bulbs work. Imagine if there were no books about light bulbs, no Google results on light bulbs, and no one had thought to keep a record of how the light bulb works. It would be really annoying to have to go through all that evolution of thought and ideas to get to the invention of the light bulb again. Those thousands and thousands of years it took to get from early humans making fire to the moment Thomas Edison cried 'Eureka!' Thousands of years to repeat all over again, with all of us just sitting in the dark.

I'm having a panic attack just thinking about it. Luckily, there's a lot of information recorded about the light bulb – 74,000,000 results on Google alone – so fingers crossed, our light bulb knowledge is safe.

However, what this vision of a terrifying bulb-free future shows us is that it's really important to record important things so we don't forget them, so we aren't doomed to repeat ourselves and so we can build on them. This is something that's proved really hard for women.

Women's voices have been systematically silenced through-out history, so when it comes to women's ideas, they very often haven't been recorded at all. If they have been recorded, they haven't been given the same platform as men, and often they have been recorded inaccurately. Nowhere is this more evident than in the speeches women have made.

A lot of history is made up of speeches. Speeches about big ideas, celebratory speeches, rousing speeches to inspire soldiers to fight to the death, comic speeches to help us see the ridiculousness in life. From Jesus to Winston Churchill to Trump, I'm sure you can finish off these sentences ...

'Turn the _____ cheek.'
'We'll fight them on the _____.'
'Make America _____ again.'

We've been raised with their words ringing in our ears. We can recall them verbatim, their soundbites, their ideas – even if we don't like them! We can take their ideas and build on them. We can stand on the shoulders of giant historical men.

There have been around 55 billion women. Fifty-five billion women's lives lived on earth. That's worth more than one book. Those are a lot of shoulders we don't get to stand on. A lot of ideas we don't get to build on. A lot of things we are doomed to repeat. When it comes to women's rhetoric it's like we are reinventing the light bulb every day.

Women's words from history are not ringing in our ears. Unless you're the type of person who loves researching suffrage speeches, you are unlikely to know many soundbites from women pre-2014. One, maybe? Two, at a push? It's not that women haven't been giving speeches – even though they were actively discouraged – it's that history hasn't been listening.

I first started researching women's speeches in 2008, during my Master's degree. This was the tail end of third-wave feminism, post post-feminism (a period of time from the 90s to the early noughties when feminism was kinda cool again). So, post-Thatcher, Ladettes and Girl Power, and I could find just one book, *Available Means: An Anthology of Women's Rhetoric(s)*. That's not enough books.

I probably don't need to tell you this, even if you've never picked up a book on historic speeches before, but most books about historic speeches are filled with men. There are some token women thrown in, sometimes, but if an alien came down to earth and that alien decided to do some research on Amazon, they would get the impression that women only really began having something to say in the 1970s, and only in large numbers in 2014. But, even with women being forced to live second-class lives throughout much of history, that's simply not the case. Instead, women have been very vocal, going out of their way to articulate their opinions and ideas, even though noisy women have been considered very unattractive.

When I was growing up throughout the 80s and 90s, I witnessed a lot of men in real life and on the telly using their hands to imitate a gossiping woman, and 'yap yap yap-ping' to put talkative women down. Loud, opinionated women were annoying. They were to be ridiculed and ignored, mimicked like a squawking goose. A hand shaped into a beak frantically snapping up and down, 'yap' hooted repeatedly like an aggressive bird. A group of loud women were literally a gaggle of geese.

It made no sense, because there had been a period of time during the 60s and 70s when feminist activism was prevalent, particularly with a view to changing the law; this was second-wave feminism. Due to these women, when I was a kid we already had lots of the laws we needed to be living in a feminist utopia of equality, but culture had sadly not caught up and opinionated women were still ridiculed out of the spotlight even though they had the legal right to be there.

I cannot imagine what it must have been like for squawking women before feminism, before suffrage, throughout most of history. Why would you ever want to utter your opinion? What would be the point? It was ugly, not feminine, dangerous and certainly not worth the hassle. Yet, once you do a bit of digging, you see time and time again that women would not be silenced.

Andrea Dworkin, the archetypal so-called 'killjoy' feminist, stood in front of a room of 500 men and demanded a 24-hour truce on rape. Sojourner Truth, who escaped slavery, spoke in front of an audience of white abolitionists and women's rights activists, challenging them to treat her as a woman too. They weren't talking to people who would necessarily agree with them, they weren't speaking in front of people who would even like them, but they took a risk because they believed that what they had to say had to be said – and heard.

I am in awe of all the noisy birds. The hooting ladies. The banshees, moaners, cacklers, gaggles, the loud, obnoxious, annoying women. The women who make themselves vulnerable by standing up and saying what they think. Who, in many cases, risked their reputation, relationships, work and even their lives, whether while running for President or making a stand in the pub. I want to celebrate them with you. For us to hear them, and to know what they've said. To hear what women thought was so important to say that they took the risk of being loud, even when the chances of us ever hearing them were so small.

Right now we're in the midst of the fourth wave of feminism. This wave, like all waves, will likely fade. It's vital that we see ourselves in the context of our history as women. It's important to see how the conversation has been shaped over the centuries. How we have got to this point. We need to know what women have said before us so we can stand on the shoulders of giants and not be doomed to repeat ourselves.

And we can't just pick the women we like. The women we agree with. The safe women. Or the obvious women. History is useless if we only look at the pretty bits. I'm very suspicious of anyone who says a woman should not be allowed to talk. We've had a history of being silenced. If a woman is brave enough to talk, we should be brave enough to listen.

So in this book you won't just hear from the obvious and acceptable women, though there are some of them in here too. You'll hear from the maligned, the misunderstood, the dangerous, the weirdos, the funny, angry women of all classes and backgrounds. This is a pluralist collage of women's ideas, and I hope that the differences and similarities of these speeches, when placed next to each other, will help us gain a new perspective on our own lives, and the right to speak up and be heard.

This book is inspired by a show I created with my all-women performance group, Gaggle. Our show, *Yap Yap Yap*, started as part of Outset's fig-2 exhibition in the Institute of Contemporary Arts, London, 2015. The show has a cast of brilliant actors joined by special guests including singer and activist Charlotte Church, actor and activist Nicola Coughlan, telly legend Su Pollard and comedian Shazia Mirza. Since then it's been to Swansea's Volcano Theatre as part of their Troublemakers Festival and back to a sell-out show at London's Royal Festival Hall as part of WOW – Women of the World Festival 2018.

Even in this huge hall, it didn't feel like we'd done these speeches and what they can teach us justice. So, this book is a version of the *Yap Yap Yap* show that anyone, anywhere, can have at home or in their library or online. We can all have it and go to it when we need reminding that we are not alone, floating in time and space. That we share frustrations, inspiration, jokes and despair with women across history and the globe. That our ideas don't have to be forgotten and can be built on. That we can be heard and listen to each other.

CHAPTER 1

SAY IT

'When I'm hungry, I eat. When I'm thirsty, I drink. When I feel like saying something, I say it.'
Madonna

I once spent an entire EasyJet flight from London to Berlin furiously writing a speech in my head that I was going to deliver to this disgrace of a stag do behind me. They had been abusive to the cabin crew, would not stop kicking the chairs of my 70-year-old parents and were just the worst.

The speech was a beauty. It covered the historical and cultural context of toxic masculinity. There was alliteration and clever wordplay. It was devastatingly honest about where the stags rated on the scale of attractiveness, comedy and brains. This was going to rouse the entire passenger list, uniting us and restoring justice to the tiny orange plane. There would be tears, cheers and a standing ovation.

But I never said it because life's no *Bridesmaids* the movie, and rather than rapturous applause, I had visions of boos and undercover aircraft security taking me down mid rant. I've never forgotten it. Not saying something you really care about is like holding in a sneeze and not scratching an itch all at the same time. Bottling up all those thoughts and emotions that need to be expressed. Imagine if we never held back. If we took the lid off that bottle and spilled everything we wanted to say.

It doesn't have to be grandiose statements on planes, just the small stuff. What if we just say what we really mean. Say YES to everything we'd love to do, and NO to all the things we don't want to do. Everyday free speech.

No, I don't want to go see *Spider-Man*. Yes, I would like to go white water rafting. No, you've got that wrong, I definitely deserve a raise. Yes, I would love to snog you. No, how you spoke to the cabin crew is not acceptable.

In this first chapter you'll hear from some of the women who fought for our very right to speak. Margaret Fell and Sor Juana fought with the church and philosophers. Virginia Woolf fought with editors, academics and her peers. Audre Lorde battled with racists, homophobes, bigots and arseholes the world over. They even fought with themselves, wrestling with their own minds, their conscience and fears, fighting that inner critic: Why would anyone listen to me? Will people not like me if they hear what I have to say? What if I make a dick of myself?

We open with chat show queen Oprah. Her 2018 Golden Globe speech shows us why we MUST speak up. Why we need to tell our truth, 'to say something about how men and women really behave', because that's the only way we can make things change. Our stories, whether in speeches, on Twitter or in the pub, fuelled the #MeToo movement and rocked the powerful status quo. True stories broke through shame and the limitations of the law.

For these women, being able to use their voices and be heard was worth prison, banishment and worse. It was worth the risk of embarrassment, not just as a matter of fairness, not just because, as Audre Lorde says, 'silence will not protect you', but because it is a human need. We need to – like Madonna – express ourselves.

OPRAH WINFREY

(1954–)

TIME'S UP

I own way too many unauthorised Oprah Winfrey biographies. Friends buy me Oprah merch every birthday. I'm a super fan. Her career has been dedicated to speaking the unspoken, hearing the voices less heard and helping us deal with those stories. She is the very definition of outspoken.

From her beginnings in poverty in Mississippi, through breaking down the barriers of race, gender, class and abuse, in a book of women firsts and first women, she's the epitome. It was winning an oratory contest that secured her a scholarship to Tennessee State University. She was then the first black woman to host her own network chat show – the highest-rated programme of its kind in history – and became North America's first black multi-billionaire and the first black woman to own her own network. She's now one of the world's most powerful women.

She's won Emmys, Oscars and Tonys and has been given the Presidential Medal of Freedom. As she accepted another award, the Cecil B. DeMille Award for lifetime achievement, at the Golden Globes in 2018, just as the #MeToo movement was gaining global momentum, she delivered a gut-thumping speech that brought everyone to their feet.

In 1964, I was a little girl sitting on the linoleum floor of my mother's house in Milwaukee watching Anne Bancroft present the Oscar for Best Actor at the 36th Academy Awards. She opened the envelope and said five words that literally made history: 'The winner is Sidney Poitier.' Up to the stage came the most elegant man I had ever seen. I remember his tie was white, and of course his skin was black and I had never seen a black man being celebrated like that. I tried many, many times to explain what a moment like that means to a little girl, a kid watching from the cheap seats as my mom came through the door bone-tired from cleaning other people's houses. But all I can do is quote and say the explanation in Sidney's performance in *Lilies of the Field*:

'Amen, amen, amen, amen.'

In 1982, Sidney received the Cecil B. DeMille award right here at the Golden Globes and it is not lost on me that at this moment, there are some little girls watching as I became the first black woman to be given this same award. It is an – it is an honour and it is a privilege to share the evening with all of them and also with the incredible men and women who have inspired me, who challenged me, who sustained me and made my journey to this stage possible. Dennis Swanson, who took a chance on me for *A.M. Chicago*. Quincy Jones, who saw me on that show and said to Steven Spielberg, 'Yes, she is Sophia in *The Color Purple*.' Gayle, who has been the definition of what a friend is, and Stedman, who has been my rock – just a few to name.

I want to thank the Hollywood Foreign Press Association because we all know the press is under siege these days. We also know it's the insatiable dedication to uncovering the absolute truth that keeps us from turning a blind eye to corruption and to injustice. To – to tyrants and victims, and secrets and lies. I want to say that I value the press more than ever before as we try to navigate these complicated times, which brings me to this:

What I know for sure is that speaking your truth is the most powerful tool we all have.

And I'm especially proud and inspired by all the women who have felt strong enough and empowered enough to speak up and share their personal stories. Each of us in this room are celebrated because of the stories that we tell and this year we became the story.

But it's not just a story affecting the entertainment industry. It's one that transcends any culture, geography, race, religion, politics or workplace. So I want tonight to express gratitude to all the women who have endured years of abuse and assault because they, like my mother, had children to feed and bills to pay and dreams to pursue. They're the women whose names we'll never know.

They are domestic workers and farm workers. They are working in factories and they work in restaurants and they're in academia, engineering, medicine and science. They're part of the world of tech and politics and business. They're our athletes in the Olympics and they're our soldiers in the military.

And there's someone else, Recy Taylor, a name I know and I think you should know, too. In 1944, Recy Taylor was a young wife and mother walking home from a church service she'd attended in Abbeville, Alabama, when she was abducted by six armed white men, raped and left blind-folded by the side of the road coming home from church. They threatened to kill her if she ever told anyone, but her story was reported to the NAACP where a young worker by the name of Rosa Parks became the lead investigator on her case and together they sought justice. But justice wasn't an option in the era of Jim Crow. The men who tried to destroy her were never prosecuted. Recy Taylor died ten days ago, just shy of her 98th birthday. She lived, as we all have lived, too many years in a culture broken by brutally powerful men. For too long, women have not been heard or believed if they dare speak the truth to the power of those men. But their time is up. Their time is up.

Their time is up. And I just hope – I just hope that Recy Taylor died knowing that her truth, like the truth of so many other women who were tormented in those years, and are even now tormented, goes marching on. It was somewhere in Rosa Parks' heart almost 11 years later, when she made the decision to stay seated on that bus in Montgomery, and it's here with every woman who chooses to say, 'Me too.' And every man – every man who chooses to listen.

In my career, what I've always tried my best to do, whether on television or through film, is to say something about how men and women really behave.

To say how we experience shame, how we love and how we rage, how we fail, how we retreat, persevere and how we overcome. I've interviewed and portrayed people who've withstood some of the ugliest things life can throw at you, but the one quality all of them seem to share is an ability to maintain hope for a brighter morning, even during our darkest nights. So I want all the girls watching here, now, to know that a new day is on the horizon! And when that new day finally dawns, it will be because of a lot of magnif-icent women, many of whom are right here in this room tonight, and some pretty phenomenal men, fighting hard to make sure that they become the leaders who take us to the time when nobody ever has to say 'Me too' again.

VIRGINIA WOOLF
(1882–1941)
A ROOM OF ONE'S OWN

From a televisual master storyteller to a literary legend. The celebrated early 20th-century writer of novels like *Mrs Dalloway* and *Orlando*, Woolf is well known for saying:

> 'A woman must have money and a room of her own if she is to write fiction.'

Fans of Woolf will know this quote comes from an essay titled *A Room of One's Own*; you can buy it as a till-point gift book – my copy was an impulse at the counter in a record shop. What I didn't realise was that this cute essay book was actually based on a series of lectures Woolf gave at Cambridge University and that this work was basically a massive pep talk and not just academic musings.

Woolf is painfully aware of her privilege in these talks, with self-deprecating humour throughout. Her audience of students at the women's only colleges of Newnham and Girton would have been white and middle (if not upper) class, like herself. Cambridge University is still criticised today for a lack of diversity in its intake. One of their colleges didn't offer a place to any black students between 2012 and 2016, and only just over 10% of students come from a working-class background.

Many of us will be able to see ourselves in Woolf's words, lovers of cat memes will understand Woolf's love of cheeky Persian cats, but all of us who have experienced painful self-doubt in our self-expression can relate to her as well. The fear of rejection if we are truly ourselves. You will recognise the battle Woolf has with her own inner good girl – *The Angel in the House.*

To tell you my story – it is a simple one. You have only got to figure to yourselves a girl in a bedroom with a pen in her hand. She had only to move that pen from left to right – from ten o'clock to one. Then it occurred to her to do what is simple and cheap enough after all – to slip a few of those pages into an envelope, fix a penny stamp in the corner and drop the envelope into the red box at the corner.

It was thus that I became a journalist; and my effort was rewarded on the first day of the following month – a very glorious day it was for me – by a letter from an editor containing a cheque for one pound ten shillings and sixpence.

But to show you how little I deserve to be called a professional woman, how little I know of the struggles and difficulties of such lives, I have to admit that instead of spending that sum upon bread and butter, rent, shoes and stockings, or butcher's bills, I went out and bought a cat – a beautiful cat, a Persian cat, which very soon involved me in bitter disputes with my neighbours.

What could be easier than to write articles and to buy Persian cats with the profits? But wait a moment. Articles have to be about something. Mine, I seem to remember, was about a novel by a famous man. And while I was writing this review, I discovered that if I were going to review books I should need to do battle with a certain phantom. And the phantom was a woman, and when I came to know her better, I called her after the heroine of a famous poem, *The Angel in the House*.

It was she who used to come between me and my paper when I was writing reviews. It was she who bothered me and wasted my time and so tormented me that at last I killed her.

You who come of a younger and happier generation may not have heard of her – you may not know what I mean by the 'Angel in the House'. I will describe her as shortly as I can. She was intensely sympathetic. She was immensely charming. She was utterly unselfish. She excelled in the difficult arts of family life. She sacrificed herself daily. If there was chicken, she took the leg; if there was a draught she sat in it – in short, she was so constituted that she never had a mind or a wish of her own, but preferred to sympathise always with the minds and wishes of others.

Above all – I need not say it – she was pure. Her purity was supposed to be her chief beauty – her blushes, her great grace. In those days every house had its Angel. And when I came to write, I encountered her with the very first words. The shadow of her wings fell on my page; I heard the rustling of her skirts in the room.

Directly I took my pen in my hand to review that novel by a famous man, she slipped behind me and whispered: 'My dear, you are a young woman. You are writing about a book that has been written by a man. Be sympathetic; be tender; flatter; deceive; use all the arts and wiles of our sex. Never let anybody guess that you have a mind of your own. Above all, be pure.' And she made as if to guide my pen.

I now record the one act for which I take some credit to myself, though the credit rightly belongs to some excellent ancestors of mine who left me a certain sum of money – so that it was not necessary for me to depend solely on charm for my living. I turned upon her and caught her by the throat. I did my best to kill her. My excuse, if I were to be had up in a court of law, would be that I acted in self-defence. Had I not killed her she would have killed me. She would have plucked the heart out of my writing.

MARGARET FELL

(1614–1702)

WOMEN'S SPEAKING JUSTIFIED

From the seat of power in London to the depths of northern England in Cumbria, a revolution was occurring in the 1600s, led by a feminist pioneer. Fell helped found the Religious Society of Friends (Quakers). She was imprisoned twice for practising her faith and is known as the Mother of Quakerism.

Let's be honest: this isn't the easiest passage to read. It's written in olde worlde English and constantly references the Bible (I've taken the chapter and verse references out for you). It's as unreadable to us as a load of hashtag meme-filled tweets would be to Fell. But she sparked the first flame that resulted in us being able to witter away on Twitter.

Fell argued passionately and fearlessly that women should be allowed to speak and be heard in church, and in 1666 she released a pamphlet titled *Women's Speaking Justified*, from which the extract below is taken.

You might want to be heard in Parliament, or in the media, at work or on Instagram, but back then the church was the place you needed to be heard to make a difference in your community. It was the place to change things, to start a revolution. Fell argued God was on women's side, using scripture to argue her case like a crack lawyer.

Whereas it hath been an Objection in the minds of many, and several times hath been objected by the Clergy, or Ministers, and others, against Women's speaking in the Church; and so consequently may be taken, that they are condemned for meddling in the things of God; the ground of which Objection, is taken from the Apostle's words, which he Writ in his first Epistle to the Corinthians. And also what he writ to Timothy in the first Epistle.

But how far they wrong the Apostle's intentions in these Scriptures, we shall shew clearly when we come to them in their course and order. But first let me lay down how God himself hath manifested his Will and Mind concerning Women, and unto Women.

And first, when God created Man in his own Image: in the Image of God created he them, Male and Female: and God blessed them, and God said unto them, Be fruitful, and multiply: Here God joyns them together in his own Image.

God hath put no such difference between the Male and Female as men would make.

And so let this serve to stop that opposing Spirit that would limit the Power and Spirit of the Lord Jesus, whose Spirit is poured upon all flesh, both Sons and Daughters, now in his Resurrection; and since that the Lord God in the Creation, when he made man in his own Image, he made them male and female; and since that Christ Jesus, as the Apostle saith, was made of a Woman, and the power of the Highest overshadowed her, and the holy Ghost came upon her, and the holy thing that was born of her, was called the Son of God, and when he was upon the Earth, he manifested his love, and his will, and his mind, both to the Woman of Samaria, and Martha, and Mary her Sister, and several others, as hath been shewed; and after his Resurrection also manifested himself unto them first of all, even before he ascended unto his Father.

Now when Jesus was risen, the first day of the week, he appeared first unto Mary Magdalene. And thus the Lord Jesus hath manifested himself and his Power, without respect of Persons, and so let all mouths be stopt that would limit him, whose Power and Spirit is infinite, that is pouring it upon all flesh.

And thus much in answer to these two Scriptures, which have been such a stumbling block, that the ministers of Darkness have made such a mountain of; But the Lord is removing all this, and taking it out of the way.

SOR JUANA
(1648–1695)
THE REPLY/LA RESPUESTA

As Fell's pamphlet caused a stir in England, on the other side of the world another prototype feminist was turning 18. Sor or Sister Juana was born into Spanish-ruled Mexico, and she has become known as the first feminist of the Americas.

Destined to be an overachiever, Sor Juana was fluent in Latin as a child and known for bossing it in philosophy as a teen. Like many clever women throughout history, she joined a nunnery, where she would have more freedom to write about philosophy and, in her case, misogyny. She attracted big thinkers of her time and opened up her quarters as an intellectual salon. This behaviour was not the norm and didn't go unnoticed, and she was advised by powerful men in the church to give up her writing and concentrate on praying.

In response to her critics she penned The Reply, and argues, with humour, the case for why women should be able to learn, teach and lead. She does it in this extract by summoning up centuries of legendary women who came before her, and writing the essential Who's Who of the women of antiquity.

If studies, my Lady, be merits (for indeed I see them extolled as such in men), in me they are no such thing: I study because I must. If they be a failing, I believe for the same reason that the fault is none of mine. Yet withal, I live always so wary of myself that neither in this nor in anything else do I trust my own judgment. And so I entrust the decision to your supreme skill and straightway submit to whatever sentence you may pass, posing no objection or reluctance, for this has been no more than a simple account of my inclination to letters.

I confess also that, while in truth this inclination has been such that, as I said before, I had no need of exemplars, nevertheless the many books that I have read have not failed to help me, both in sacred as well as secular letters. For there I see a Deborah issuing laws, military as well as political, and governing the people among whom there were so many learned men. I see the exceedingly knowledgeable Queen of Sheba, so learned she dares to test the wisdom of the wisest of all wise men with riddles, without being rebuked for it; indeed, on this very account she is to become judge of the unbelievers. I see so many and such significant women: some adorned with the gift of prophecy, like an Abigail; others, of persuasion, like Esther; others, of piety like Rahab; others, of perseverance, like Anna [Hannah] the mother of Samuel; and others, infinitely more, with other kinds of qualities and virtues.

When I consider the Gentiles, the first I meet are the Sibyls, chosen to prophesy the essential mysteries of our Faith in such beautiful and elegant verses that they stupefy the imagination. I see a woman such as Minerva, daughter of great Jupiter and mistress of all the wisdom of Athens, adored as goddess of the sciences. I see one Polla Argentaria, who helped Lucan, her husband, to write the *Battle of Pharsalia*. I see the daughter of the divine Tiresias, more learned still than her father. I see, too, such a woman as Zenobia, queen of the Palmyrians, as wise as she was courageous. Again, I see an Arete, daughter of Aristippus, most learned. A Nicostrata, inventor of Latin letters and most erudite in the Greek. An Aspasia Miletia, who taught philosophy and rhetoric and was the teacher of the philosopher Pericles. An Hypatia, who taught astrology and lectured for many years in Alexandria. A Leontium, who won over the philosopher Theophrastus and proved him wrong. A Julia, a Corinna, a Cornelia; and, in sum, the vast throng of women who merited titles and earned renown: now as Greeks, again as Muses, and yet again as Pythonesses.

For what were they all but learned women, who were considered, celebrated, and indeed venerated as such in Antiquity? Without mentioning still others, of whom the books are full; for I see the Egyptian Catherine, lecturing and refuting all the learning of the most learned men of Egypt. I see a Gertrude read, write, and teach. And seeking no more examples far from home, I see my own most holy mother Paula, learned in the Hebrew, Greek, and Latin tongues and most expert in the interpretation of the Scriptures. What wonder then can it be that, though her chronicler was no less than the unequalled Jerome, the Saint found himself scarcely worthy of the task, for with that lively gravity and energetic effectiveness with which only he can express himself, he says: 'If all the parts of my body were tongues, they would not suffice to proclaim the learning and virtues of Paula.' Blessilla, a widow, earned the same praises, as did the luminous virgin Eustochium, both of them daughters of the Saint herself [Paula]; and indeed Eustochium was such that for her knowledge she was hailed as a World Prodigy. Fabiola, also a Roman, was another most learned in Holy Scripture. Proba Falconia, a Roman woman, wrote an elegant book of centos, joining together verses from Virgil, on the mysteries of our holy Faith. Our Queen Isabella, wife of Alfonso X, is known to have written on astrology – without mentioning others, whom I omit so as not merely to copy what others have said (which is a vice I have always detested): Well then, in our own day there thrive the great Christina Alexandra, Queen of Sweden, as learned as she is brave and generous; and too those most excellent ladies, the Duchess of Aveyro and the Countess of Villaumbrosa.

The venerable Dr Arce (worthy professor of Scripture, known for his virtue and learning), in his *For the Scholar of the Bible*, raises this question: '*Is it permissible for women to apply themselves to the study and indeed the interpretation, of the Holy Bible?'* And in opposition he presents the verdicts passed by many saints, particularly the words of [Paul] the Apostle: *'Let women keep silence in the churches: for it is not permitted them to speak,'* etc. Arce then presents differing verdicts, including this passage addressed to Titus, again spoken by the Apostle: *'The aged women, in like manner, in holy attire [...] teaching well,'*; and he gives other interpretations from the Fathers of the Church. Arce at last resolves, in his prudent way, that women are not allowed to lecture publicly in the universities or to preach from the pulpits, but that studying, writing and teaching privately is not only permitted but most beneficial and useful to them.

Clearly, of course, he does not mean by this that all women should do so, but only those whom God may have seen fit to endow with special virtue and prudence, and who are very mature and erudite and possess the necessary talents and requirements for such a sacred occupation. And so just is this distinction that not only women, who are held to be so incompetent, but also men, who simply because they are men think themselves wise, are to be prohibited from the interpretation of the Sacred Word, save when they are most learned, virtuous, of amenable intellect and inclined to the good. For when the reverse is true, I believe, numerous sectarians are produced, and this has given rise to numerous heresies. For there are many who study only to become ignorant, especially those of arrogant, restless, and prideful spirits, fond of innovations in the Law (the very thing that rejects all innovation). And so they are not content until, for the sake of saying what no one before them has said, they speak heresy. Of such men as these the Holy Spirit says: '*For wisdom will not enter into a malicious soul.*' For them, more harm is worked by knowledge than by ignorance. A wit once observed that he who knows no Latin is not an utter fool, but he who does know it has met the prerequisites. And I might add that he is made a perfect fool (if foolishness can attain perfection) by having studied his bit of philosophy and theology and by knowing something of languages.

For with that he can be foolish in several sciences and tongues; a great fool cannot be contained in his mother tongue alone.

AUDRE LORDE

(1934–1992)

THE TRANSFORMATION OF SILENCE

Three hundred years after Sor Juana, and another overachiever, Lorde, would address a Lesbian Literature Panel in Chicago in 1977. She delivered this iconic paper, written in the aftermath of her own cancer scare. Lorde considered herself to exist outside the realms of 'acceptable' women. Black, lesbian, born to immigrant parents in Harlem, New York, Lorde went to a high school for the intellectually gifted and became an internationally recognised poet, activist and intellectual.

Lorde was critical of mainstream feminists for not representing queer women and women of colour. She expressed outrage in her work at injustices in society, in the knowledge that it was not considered attractive or acceptable to display anger. This gets to the heart of this chapter – we must say what we think, in spite of what society deems appropriate, even if we think the plane might boo, if it's important to us. Lorde knew it was essential, in fact existential, and in this extract she explains how there's no point staying silent, because swallowing 'your tyrannies' will cause you to 'sicken and die' from them, still in silence.

I have come to believe over and over again that what is most important to me must be spoken, made verbal and shared, even at the risk of having it bruised and misunderstood. That the speaking profits me, beyond any other effect. I am standing here as a Black lesbian poet, and the meaning of all that waits upon the fact that I am still alive, and might not have been. Less than two months ago I was told by two doctors, one female and one male, that I would have to have breast surgery, and that there was a 60 to 80% chance that the tumour was malignant. Between that telling and the actual surgery, there was a three-week period of the agony of an involuntary reorganisation of my entire life. The surgery was completed and the growth was benign.

But within those three weeks, I was forced to look upon myself and my living with a harsh and urgent clarity that has left me still shaken but much stronger. This is a situation faced by many women, by some of you here today. Some of what I experienced during that time has helped elucidate for me much of what I feel concerning the transformation of silence into language and action.

In becoming forcibly and essentially aware of my mortality, and of what I wished and wanted for my life, however short it might be, priorities and omissions became strongly etched in a merciless light, and what I most regretted were my silences. Of what had I *ever* been afraid? To question or to speak as I believed could have meant pain or death. But we all hurt in so many different ways, all the time, and pain will either change or end.

Death, on the other hand, is the final silence. And that might be coming quickly, now, without regard for whether I had ever spoken what needed to be said, or had only betrayed myself into small silences, while I planned someday to speak, or waited for someone else's words.

And I began to recognise a source of power within myself that comes from the knowledge that while it is most desirable not to be afraid, learning to put fear into a perspective gave me great strength.

I was going to die, if not sooner then later, whether or not I had ever spoken myself. My silences had not protected me. Your silence will not protect you. But for every real word spoken, for every attempt I had ever made to speak those truths for which I am still seeking, I had made contact with other women while we examined the words to fit a world in which we all believed, bridging our differences. And it was the concern and caring of all those women which gave me strength and enabled me to scrutinise the essentials of my living.

The women who sustained me through that period were Black and white, old and young, lesbian, bisexual, and heterosexual, and we all shared a war against the tyrannies of silence. They all gave me a strength and concern without which I could not have survived intact. Within those weeks of acute fear came the knowledge – within the war we are all waging with the forces of death, subtle and otherwise, conscious or not – I am not only a casualty, I am also a warrior.

What are the words you do not yet have? What do you need to say?

What are the tyrannies you swallow day by day and attempt to make your own, until you will sicken and die of them, still in silence? Perhaps for some of you here today, I am the face of one of your fears. Because I am woman, because I am Black, because I am lesbian, because I am myself – a Black woman warrior poet doing my work – come to ask you, are you doing yours?

And of course I am afraid, because the transformation of silence into language and action is an act of self-revelation, and that always seems fraught with danger. But my daughter, when I told her of our topic and my difficulty with it, said, 'Tell them about how you're never really a whole person if you remain silent, because there's always that one little piece inside you that wants to be spoken out, and if you keep ignoring it, it gets madder and madder and hotter and hotter, and if you don't speak it out one day it will just up and punch you in the mouth from the inside.'

In the cause of silence, each of us draws the face of her own fear – fear of contempt, of censure, or some judgment, or recognition, of challenge, of annihilation. But most of all, I think, we fear the visibility without which we cannot truly live. Within this country where racial difference creates a constant, if unspoken, distortion of vision, Black women have on one hand always been highly visible, and so, on the other hand, have been rendered invisible through the depersonalisation of racism. Even within the women's movement, we have had to fight, and still do, for that very visibility which also renders us most vulnerable, our Blackness. For to survive in the mouth of this dragon we call america, we have had to learn this first and most vital lesson – that we were never meant to survive. Not as human beings. And neither were most of you here today, Black or not. And that visibility which makes us most vulnerable is that which also is the source of our greatest strength. Because the machine will try to grind you into dust anyway, whether or not we speak. We can sit in our corners mute forever while our sisters and our selves are wasted, while our children are distorted and destroyed, while our earth is poisoned; we can sit in our safe corners mute as bottles, and we will still be no less afraid.

In my house this year we are celebrating the feast of Kwanza, the African–American festival of harvest which begins the day after Christmas and lasts for seven days. There are seven principles of Kwanza, one for each day. The first principle is *Umoja*, which means unity, the decision to strive for and maintain unity in self and community. The principle for yesterday, the second day, was *Kujichagulia* – self-determination – the decision to define ourselves, name ourselves, and speak for ourselves, instead of being defined and spoken for by others. Today is the third day of Kwanza, and the principle for today is *Ujima* – collective work and responsibility – the decision to build and maintain ourselves and our communities together and to recognise and solve our problems together.

Each of us is here now because in one way or another we share a commitment to language and to the power of language, and to the reclaiming of that language which has been made to work against us. In the transformation of silence into language and action, it is vitally necessary for each one of us to establish or examine her function in that transformation and to recognise her role as vital within that transformation.

For those of us who write, it is necessary to scrutinise not only the truth of what we speak, but the truth of that language by which we speak it. For others, it is to share and spread also those words that are meaningful to us. But primarily for us all, it is necessary to teach by living and speaking those truths which we believe and know beyond understanding. Because in this way alone we can survive, by taking part in a process of life that is creative and continuing, that is growth.

And it is never without fear – of visibility, of the harsh light of scrutiny and perhaps judgment, of pain, of death. But we have lived through all of those already, in silence, except death. And I remind myself all the time now that if I were to have been born mute, or had maintained an oath of silence my whole life long for safety, I would still have suffered, and I would still die. It is very good for establishing perspective.

And where the words of women are crying to be heard, we must each of us recognise our responsibility to seek those words out, to read them and share them and examine them in their pertinence to our lives. That we not hide behind the mockeries of separations that have been imposed upon us and which so often we accept as our own. For instance, 'I can't possibly teach Black women's writing – their experience is so different from mine.' Yet how many years have you spent teaching Plato and Shakespeare and Proust? Or another, 'She's a white woman and what could she possibly have to say to me?' Or, 'She's a lesbian, what would my husband say, or my chairman?' Or again, 'This woman writes of her sons and I have no children.' And all the other endless ways in which we rob ourselves of ourselves and each other.

We can learn to work and speak when we are afraid in the same way we have learned to work and speak when we are tired. For we have been socialised to respect fear more than our own needs for language and definition, and while we wait in silence for that final luxury of fearlessness, the weight of that silence will choke us.

The fact that we are here and that I speak these words is an attempt to break that silence and bridge some of those differences between us, for it is not difference which immobilises us, but silence. And there are so many silences to be broken.

CHAPTER 2

YOUR BODY

'The beauty myth is always actually prescribing behaviour and not appearance.'
Naomi Wolf, *The Beauty Myth*

When I posted on Instagram about having an ectopic pregnancy last December, lots of friends I thought I knew well got in touch saying the same had happened to them, but they had never told anyone. If you've suffered anything like this in silence you have nothing to be ashamed of, and this is why …

Your body is a battleground. On one side there is you, you in your body, being brilliant, living your life. On the other side is stigmatisation, control and policing. And in the middle is a big old cloud of shame:

- Stigma around perfectly normal bodily functions like breast feeding in public, period sex and when stuff doesn't go to plan, anything from HPV to miscarriage.

- Control of size, shape, colour, shade, body hair, where you are expected to fit into a narrow box of what is deemed 'beauty'. In May 2019 the Mental Health Foundation released the results of a study they did with over 4,500 people in the UK. They discovered that one in 10 women said they had self-harmed or 'deliberately hurt themselves' because of their body image.
- And actual policing, when your body is subject to strict laws, and you can end up imprisoned or worse, like in some countries, with abortion and hair covering.

It's exhausting. Generations of women tip-toeing around all of this. It doesn't just literally stop us from living freely, it stops us from talking honestly about our lives, from sharing the information we need to make smart choices about our bodies. Which is why we are more likely to be underprescribed painkillers, and more likely to have our heart attacks misdiagnosed.

As we push to change all of this, history teaches us to be vigilant. Abortion may be set to become legalised in Northern Ireland, but we can see how easily these rights can be taken back across the Atlantic as they were in Arkansas in 2019. In this chapter we hear from two women's health advocates – Margaret Sanger and Sarah Weddington – both of whom fought for women to have the right to choose when they have a baby.

We hear from Masih Alinejad how she is attacked with the word 'ugly' for campaigning against the policing of women's hair in Iran. How long before Miley Cyrus, the artist and sex worker Annie Sprinkle radically reclaimed her own sexualised body in an extract from her most famous piece of performance art. We start and end this chapter with women who are promoting radical self love. *The Good Place*'s Jameela Jamil telling a gathering at the House of Commons that she's not taking media criticism any more and artist Kelli Jean Drinkwater's viral TED talk on the real elephant in the room.

JAMEELA JAMIL

(1986–)

BODY CONFIDENCE AWARDS

Jamil's story is now a familiar one we often hear about women in the public eye. We discover that these brilliant young things gracing our telly screens and airwaves are having a torturous time because of the incredible scrutiny over their looks.

Since going from UK broadcaster to international actor in *The Good Place*, Jamil has become a loud and active voice to try and change just that. To change the media and representation, calling for diversity and a celebration of difference.

In 2014 she took to the stage at the House of Commons to tell those gathered there for the Body Confidence Awards that from now on, she refuses to take it any more.

Last year I was given the huge privilege of making history as the first woman ever to host the official chart on BBC Radio 1, solo. In all of its 50 years on air. And it was something that I took really seriously. [I was] passionate about it. I thought I really have something to prove, I really want to show the nation that people don't just switch off as soon as they hear a woman's voice in authority. And then, three months later, by some miracle, it came out that I had managed to gain 200,000 listeners almost on my show.

On that same day the papers decided to ignore the fact that that had happened, and instead ran a wonderful piece about the fact that I had gained not 200,000 listeners on a radio show, but instead two dress sizes. That was the entire focus of the pieces that I saw online and on magazines, and they were accompanied with some excellent photographs, a lot of my bum.

And I found it really upsetting, because I felt like I had done something of some worth. And, in the slightest way, paved a bit of a path for women in media, and it was being so magnificently ignored, and I felt like I was being dragged down and humiliated just because I didn't do that as a size 10.

It broke my heart, because my entire worth as a broadcaster, more importantly as a woman, was being measured with a weighing scale.

But I'm sorry, I refuse, and I cannot be told or pressured to believe that I owe it to anybody to be a particular shape or size. We are all supposed to be different.

I think it's sad that we forget that our bodies are miracles. And it's so sad to watch how we are held back by this invisible shadow that is looming over us, and it's one we ourselves perpetuate every day.

So, I stand here today and say, pardon me if I will always wobble when I walk. Pardon me if I let my face wrinkle and enjoy my smile lines because they show that I have laughed. And pardon me if I have enough stretch marks on my bottom to look like an A-Z of London. And finally, pardon me if I want the daughter that I may have one day to grow up wanting a good heart, a good mind and a good life, and not a fucking thigh gap.

MASIH ALINEJAD

(1976-)

UGLY DUCKLING

From garments that empower to garments that are forced upon you. Alinejad is the founder of My Stealthy Freedom, the online movement where women would remove their hijab and let the wind flow through their hair, many in Iran where it is illegal to do so. She is not opposed to the hijab, but she thinks it should be a choice.

Alinejad grew up in rural poverty, her mother unable to read or write. She was just two when revolution took hold of her country and the compulsory hijab came to be. At 19, after she was arrested in Iran for anti-government activity, she was told by a judge that he had enough evidence to execute her. Undeterred, she has continued to rebel, gaining global human rights and journalism awards. She is now in self-exile in New York.

Addressing the Women in the World 2019 annual summit, Alinejad told the audience about the power of the word 'ugly'.

So one day I was in London because of my campaign and what I had been doing. I got attacked by a pro-regime guy in London Airport. He called me, 'Ugly woman. You're ruining the image of Iran.' And I said, 'Wait a minute. I'm not ruining the image of Iran. I'm ruining the image of the oppressors. And this is the Islamic Republic ruining the image of Iran, not me and the women who are protesting against the oppressive laws.'

So he was not convinced. That didn't bother me. What bothered me: he called me ugly. This is the way that actually they want to patronise women, they want to attack women, they want to keep us silent. You know, from Saudi Arabia. They bully you. They think if they say you're ugly, you're going to feel miserable and cry.

So what I did, I took my camera, because I knew that I'm the most beautiful woman in the world. I ran after the guy and I said ... [Responding to audience reaction] No, honestly. Why I say I'm the most beautiful, because in the eyes of my son I'm a beautiful mother. In the eyes of my mother I'm a beautiful daughter. In the eyes of my husband I'm a beautiful wife. Never let people tell you you're ugly.

And the government call me ugly duckling. They don't know even the end of the story of the ugly duckling.

So I went ... No, listen, this is the important part. I ran after that guy, I took my camera and I said to the guy, 'You called me ugly. Repeat yourself in front of my camera.' Guess what happened? He couldn't! So I won the battle. So I shared my story with the Iranian people and I launched my own version of the #MeToo movement in Iran. I said, any time you're being harassed, you're being attacked, you're being bullied, use your mobile. Because you go to the judiciary system, they put the blame on women. If you don't put a headscarf on yourself, then they blame you. You're being raped? It's your fault. So use your mobile phone and film them.

So now women are filming the harassers, the people who are attacking them, the morality police, and they send the videos to me. One of the women sent a video – it got nine million views. The supreme leader of Iran doesn't get that much views. The president of Iran doesn't get ... That shows the power of ordinary women. That shows, they kicked me out from Iran, but I am there. Because of the millions of Iranian women who are powerful enough to be warriors rather than victims.

MARGARET SANGER

(1879–1966)

MORALITY OF BIRTH CONTROL

Sanger is the original sexpert. She penned columns for a socialist newspaper, then published *What Every Girl Should Know* a hundred years ago. She taught your great-great-great-grandma how to have sex. That would be radical enough, but she went much further.

She was embedded in working-class and immigrant communities in early 20th-century New York, witnessing how women's health provision, or lack of it, was ruining lives. Sanger's organisation, the American Birth Control League, evolved into today's Planned Parenthood Federation. Though as you'll see below, Sanger had some problematic views on different categories of women who are more or less responsible than others.

This speech was banned. Sanger's magazine *Woman Rebel* was banned. She opened the first birth control clinic in the US and was imprisoned. The first birth control conference in the US, at which she was supposed to be speaking, was closed down by the police. But, just five days later, in November 1921, she took to the stage at the Park Theatre in New York City and gave this speech.

The one issue upon which there seems to be most uncertainty and disagreement exists in the moral side of the subject of birth control. It seemed only natural for us to call together scientists, educators, members of the medical profession and the theologians of all denominations to ask their opinion upon this uncertain and important phase of the controversy. Letters were sent to the most eminent men and women in the world. We asked in this letter the following questions:

1. Is overpopulation a menace to the peace of the world?

2. Would the legal dissemination of scientific birth control information through the medium of clinics by the medical profession be the most logical method of checking the problem of overpopulation?

3. Would knowledge of birth control change the moral attitude of men and women towards the marriage bond or lower the moral standards of the youth of the country?

4. Do you believe that knowledge which enables parents to limit their families will make for human happiness, and raise the moral, social and intellectual standards of population?

We sent such a letter not only to those who, we thought, might agree with us, but we sent it also to our known opponents. Most of these people answered. Everyone who answered did so with sincerity and courtesy, with the exception of one group whose reply to this important question as demonstrated at the Town Hall last Sunday evening was a disgrace to liberty-loving people, and to all traditions we hold dear in the United States. I believed that the discussion of the moral issue was one which did not solely belong to theologians and to scientists, but belonged to the people. And because I believed that the people of this country may and can discuss this subject with dignity and with intelligence I desired to bring them together, and to discuss it in the open.

When one speaks of moral, one refers to human conduct. This implies action of many kinds, which in turn depends upon the mind and the brain. So that in speaking of morals one must remember that there is a direct connection between morality and brain development. Conduct is said to be action in pursuit of ends, and if this is so, then we must hold that irresponsibility and recklessness in our actions is immoral, while responsibility and forethought put into action for the benefit of the individual and the race becomes in the highest sense the finest kind of morality.

We know that every advance that woman has made in the last half century has been made with opposition, all of which has been based upon the grounds of immorality.

When women fought for higher education, it was said that this would cause her to become immoral and she would lose her place in the sanctity of the home. When women asked for the franchise it was said that this would lower her standard of morals, that it was not fit that she should meet with and mix with the members of the opposite sex, but we notice that there was no objection to her meeting with the same members of the opposite sex when she went to church.

The church has ever opposed the progress of women on the ground that her freedom would lead to immorality. We ask the church to have more confidence in women. We ask the opponents of this movement to reverse the methods of the church, which aims to keep women moral by keeping them in fear and in ignorance, and to inculcate into them a higher and truer morality based upon knowledge. And ours is the morality of knowledge. If we cannot trust woman with the knowledge of her own body, then I claim that two thousand years of Christian teaching has proved to be a failure.

We stand on the principle that birth control should be available to every adult man and woman. We believe that every adult man and woman should be taught the responsibility and the right use of knowledge.

We claim that a woman should have the right over her own body and to say if she shall or if she shall not be a mother, as she sees fit. We further claim that the first right of a child is to be desired. While the second right is that it should be conceived in love, and the third, that it should have a heritage of sound health.

Upon these principles the birth control movement in America stands. When it comes to discussing the methods of birth control, that is far more difficult. There are laws in this country which forbid the imparting of practical information to the mothers of the land. We claim that every mother in this country, either sick or well, has the right to the best, the safest, the most scientific information. This information should be disseminated directly to the mothers through clinics by members of the medical profession, registered nurses and registered midwives.

Our first step is to have the backing of the medical profession so that our laws may be changed, so that motherhood may be the function of dignity and choice, rather than one of ignorance and chance. Conscious control of offspring is now becoming the ideal and the custom in all civilised countries. Those who oppose it claim that however desirable it may be on economic or social grounds, it may be abused and the morals of the youth of the country may be lowered. Such people should be reminded that there are two points to be considered. First, that such control is the inevitable advance in civilisation. Every civilisation involves an increasing forethought for others, even for those yet unborn. The reckless abandonment of the impulse of the moment and the careless regard for the consequences, is not morality. The selfish gratification of temporary desire at the expense of suffering to lives that will come may seem very beautiful to some, but it is not our conception of civilisation, nor is it our concept of morality.

In the second place, it is not only inevitable, but it is right to control the size of the family for by this control and adjustment we can raise the level and the standards of the human race. While nature's way of reducing her numbers is controlled by disease, famine and war, primitive man has achieved the same results by infanticide, exposure of infants, the abandonment of children, and by abortion. But such ways of controlling population is no longer possible for us. We have attained high standards of life, and along the lines of science must we conduct such control. We must begin further back and control the beginnings of life. We must control conception. This is a better method; it is a more civilised method, for it involves not only greater forethought for others, but finally a higher sanction for the value of life itself.

Society is divided into three groups. Those intelligent and wealthy members of the upper classes who have obtained knowledge of birth control and exercise it in regulating the size of their families. They have already benefited by this knowledge, and are today considered the most respectable and moral members of the community. They have only children when they desire, and all society points to them as types that should perpetuate their kind.

The second group is equally intelligent and responsible. They desire to control the size of their families, but are unable to obtain knowledge or to put such available knowledge into practice.

The third are those irresponsible and reckless ones having little regard for the consequence of their acts, or whose religious scruples prevent their exercising control over their numbers. Many of this group are diseased, feeble-minded, and are of the pauper element dependent entirely upon the normal and fit members of society for their support. There is no doubt in the minds of all thinking people that the procreation of this group should be stopped. For if they are not able to support and care for themselves, they should certainly not be allowed to bring offspring into this world for others to look after. We do not believe that filling the earth with misery, poverty and disease is moral. And it is our desire and intention to carry on our crusade until the perpetuation of such conditions has ceased.

We desire to stop at its source the disease, poverty and feeble-mindedness and insanity which exist today, for these lower the standards of civilisation and make for race deterioration. We know that the masses of people are growing wiser and are using their own minds to decide their individual conduct. The more people of this kind we have, the less immorality shall exist. For the more responsible people grow, the higher do they and shall they attain real morality.

SARAH WEDDINGTON

(1945-)

ROE v WADE ORAL ARGUMENT

You hear it a lot during US election campaigns. 'Roe v Wade'. 'We must protect Roe v Wade.' 'We must keep Ruth Ginsburg alive so the Supreme Court doesn't roll back Roe v Wade.' It is a 1973 landmark ruling of the US Supreme Court, where they ruled that the actual Constitution protects a woman's right to have an abortion.

The case was about Norma McCorvey ('Jane Roe'), who was not able to abort her third pregnancy in the state of Texas. She was represented by lawyer Sarah Weddington. The extract below is from Weddington's opening statements to the Supreme Court on 13th December 1971. Weddington's arguments went to the heart of why abortion should be a right for every woman, because otherwise women are not free.

Mr Chief Justice, and may it please the Court: The instant case is a direct appeal from a decision of the United States District Court for the Northern District of Texas.

The court declared the Texas abortion law to be uncon-stitutional for two reasons: First, that the law was impermissibly vague; and, second, that it violated a woman's right to continue or terminate a pregnancy.

Although the court granted declaratory relief, the court denied appellants' request for injunctive relief.

The Texas law in question permits abortions to be performed only in instances where it is for the purpose of saving the life of the woman.

The case originated with the filing of two separate complaints, the first being filed on behalf of Jane Roe, an unmarried pregnant girl and the second being filed on behalf of John and Mary Doe, a married couple.

Jane Roe, the pregnant woman, had gone to several Dallas physicians seeking an abortion, but had been refused care because of the Texas law.

She filed suit on behalf of herself and all those women who have in the past, at that present time, or in the future would seek termination of a pregnancy.

In her affidavit she did state some of the reasons that she desired an abortion at the time she sought one. But, contrary to the contentions of appellee, she continued to desire the abortion. And it was not only at the time she sought the abortion that her desire was to terminate the pregnancy.

. . .

Our Texas statute provides an abortion only where it is for the purpose of saving the life of the woman.

Since the Vuitch decision was rendered, the Texas Court of Criminal Appeals – which is our highest court of criminal jurisdiction – has held that the Texas law is not vague, citing the Vuitch decision, but saying that the Texas law is more definite than the D.C. law.

So, obviously the Court of Criminal Appeals doesn't feel that the two are the same. And in the Vuitch decision, the Justices of this Court emphasised continuously that a doctor, as a matter of routine, works with the problem of what is best for the health of his patients.

We submit that a doctor is not used to being restricted to acting only when it's for the purpose of saving the life of the woman, and that health is a continuum which runs into life.

And a doctor in our State does not know whether he can perform an abortion only when death is imminent or when the woman's life would be shortened. He does not know if the death must be certain, or if it could be an increase in probability of her death.

So here, in the District, doctors are able to exercise their normal matter of judgment of whether or not the health of the woman – mental or physical – would be affected.

But, in Texas, we tell the doctor that unless he can decide whether it's necessary for the purpose of saving her life, and for no other reason, that he is subject to criminal sanctions. I think it's important to note the range of problems that could be presented to a doctor.

The court, for example, cited the instance of suicide – if a woman comes in alleging that she will commit suicide. Is it then necessary for him to do, or can he do an abortion for the purpose of saving her life?

Or, is that a situation where he has to have something more? I think all of those questions cannot be answered, at this point. This brings up the married couple in our case. The woman in that case had a neurochemical condition.

Her doctor had advised her not to get pregnant, and not to take birth control pills. She was using alternative means of birth control, but she and her husband were fearful that she would become pregnant and that, although the neurochemical condition would impair her health, evidently her doctor did not feel that she would die if she continued the pregnancy.

And certainly they were very concerned about the effects of the statute, and her physician seemed uncertain about its implications. The doctors in our State continue to feel that our law is vague. Certainly, we introduced affidavits in the lower court to that effect.

Since the time of the lower court ruling, the District Attorney in Texas has said that he considers the Federal court decision there not to be binding. And we do have a letter from him – the first thing in our Appendix to the brief – stating that he will continue to prosecute.

So the doctors in Texas, even with the Federal decision and even after the Vuitch decision, do not feel free to perform abortions. And, instead, 728 women in the first nine months after the decision went to New York for an abortion.

Texas women are coming here. It's so often the poor and the disadvantaged in Texas who are not able to escape the effect of the law.

Certainly there are many Texas women who are affected because our doctors still feel uncertain about the impact of the law, even in light of the Vuitch decision.

...

Texas, for example, it appears to us, would not allow any relief at all, even in situations where the mother would suffer perhaps serious physical or mental harm. There is certainly a great question about it.

If the pregnancy would result in the birth of a deformed or defective child, she has no relief. Regardless of the circumstances of conception, whether it was because of rape, incest, whether she is extremely immature, she has no relief.

I think it's without question that pregnancy to a woman can completely disrupt her life.

Whether she's unmarried; whether she's pursuing an education; whether she's pursuing a career; whether she has family problems; all of the problems of personal and family life for a woman, are bound up in the problem of abortion.

For example, in our State there are many schools where a woman is forced to quit if she becomes pregnant. In the City of Austin [Texas] that is true. A woman, if she becomes pregnant, and is in high school, must drop out of the regular education process. And that's true of some colleges in our State.

In the matter of employment, she often is forced to quit at an early point in her pregnancy. She has no provision for maternity leave. She has... she cannot get unemployment compensation under our laws, because the laws hold that she is not eligible for employment, being pregnant, and therefore is eligible for no unemployment compensation.

At the same time, she can get no welfare to help her at a time when she has no unemployment compensation and she's not eligible for any help in getting a job to provide for herself. There is no duty for employers to rehire women if they must drop out to carry a pregnancy to term.

And, of course, this is especially hard on the many women in Texas who are heads of their own households and must provide for their already existing children.

And, obviously, the responsibility of raising a child is a most serious one, and at times an emotional investment that must be made, cannot be denied. So, a pregnancy to a woman is perhaps one of the most determinative aspects of her life.

It disrupts her body. It disrupts her education. It disrupts her employment. And it often disrupts her entire family life.

And we feel that, because of the impact on the woman, this certainly – in as far as there are any rights which are fundamental – is a matter which is of such fundamental and basic concern to the woman involved that she should be allowed to make the choice as to whether to continue or to terminate her pregnancy.

I think the question is equally serious for the physicians of our State. They are seeking to practise medicine in what they consider the highest method of practice.

We have affidavits in the back of our brief from each of the heads of public of heads of Obstetrics and Gynaecology departments from each of our public medical schools in Texas.

And each of them points out that they were willing and interested to immediately begin to formulate methods of providing care and services for women who are pregnant and do not desire to continue the pregnancy.

ANNIE SPRINKLE

(1954–)

PUBLIC CERVIX ANNOUNCEMENT

When I first discovered Annie Sprinkle I was 18, at an amazing art college for proper weirdos called Dartington College of Arts, and was looking for women who were breaking all the taboos. I bought Sprinkle's book *Post Porn Modernist* and my parents never looked at my bookshelves in quite the same way again.

This was a book celebrating her life as a sex worker and performance artist, and included documentation of her most famous work *Public Cervix Announcement*, where she invited the audience to view her cervix through a speculum with a torch. This was the early 90s. Just before Madonna released her own book titled *Sex*, and blew the mainstream's mind. Sprinkle was demystifying the sexualised female body before anyone else, and not just in relation to sex. For her it was about empowerment and pleasure.

Sprinkle is an educator, porn producer and director, an environmentalist and sex-positive feminist. Below is an extract from *Post Porn Modernist*, Sprinkle's script from *Public Cervix Announcement*.

You may be wondering why I'm going to show you my cervix. What is this all about? There are probably 1,000 reasons. I'll just tell you three. Reason number one: a cervix is such a beautiful thing and most people go through their whole lives and never get to see one.

I'm really proud of mine, and I'd like to give that opportunity to anyone who'd like to have it.

Reason number two is, I find it's a lot of fun to show my cervix in little groups like this.

And reason number three is, I want to prove to some of the guys out there that there are absolutely no teeth inside there.

Do you all know what to look for?

(Annie holds up a diagram.)

In case you don't, I've drawn up a diagram of the female reproductive system. This is the vaginal canal. Let's all say that together, shall we? VAGINAL CANAL. This is the uterus. UTERUS. These are the Fallopian tubes. FALLOPIAN TUBES. And this is the where the cervix is located. It's represented by the light pink magic marker. I was just in Holland and I learned how to say cervix in Dutch. It's Baarmoedermond. BAARMOEDERMOND.

What you're going to look for is actually this, only smaller. The way we're going to do this is really simple. I have a standard gynaecological speculum, just like they use in the doctor's office.

(Annie inserts speculum.)

It doesn't hurt at all. It actually feels kind of cool and nice. The speculum opens up the vaginal canal. (To the audience) You can all breathe. It's just amazing how tight that pussy is after all these years. I have a flashlight here. If any of you would like to come up and take a look at the Baarmoedermond, you can. Please form a line here. You have to get down low to see it.

(Annie chats with the audience, answers questions, asks them to describe it to the rest of the audience, etc.)

(After the last person in the line has seen her cervix, Annie removes speculum.)

Wasn't that fun? I take fun and pleasure very seriously. There's so much pain and suffering in the world. I believe that we have to consciously balance those scales with as much pleasure and joy and ecstasy as we possibly can. There's a saying that I really love: 'When a butterfly flaps its wings in Japan, it can cause a hurricane in New York.' It has actually been scientifically proven that on some level we are all connected. That means that as you experience pleasure, I can feel it. And as I experience pleasure and ecstasy, the whole universe feels it, too. That's why my motto is, let there be pleasure on earth and let it begin with me.

We're going to take an intermission. That will give you all time to come up and use the toilet, if you want to. I'm going to stay up here. I'll be doing 'Tits On Your Head Polaroids'. They are $5. If you want to come up and have your picture taken with my tits on your head, please do. You can take it home with you as a little souvenir.

Thank you.

INTERMISSION

KELLI JEAN DRINKWATER

(1980-)

THE FEAR OF FAT – THE REAL ELEPHANT IN THE ROOM

Just as exposure to our bodies, like Sprinkle offers us, can empower us and give us pleasure, exposure to different beauty ideals and different bodies can make us happier with our own. I'm fat, and I have spent the past few years dedicating myself to making sure I never let that hold me back.

Psychologist and author of *Fat is a Feminist Issue* Susie Orbach once told me that we need to expose ourselves to bodies that look like ours and our friends' in order to be happier. I got straight on my phone and culled my Instagram. I went looking for women who looked like me, and within months my brain had changed. I had grown compassion for my body, I had begun to accept my body.

Drinkwater is an Australian artist and activist, dealing in radical body politics. In 2016 she made this TED talk at the Sydney Opera House, challenging the audience with the opener 'I don't know if any of you noticed, but I am FAT.' She goes on to explain how there is systematic oppression of fat people, how she combatted it with acts like founding her own fat synchronised swimming team called AquaPorko, and she dares us to celebrate our bodies.

I don't know if any of you noticed, but I am FAT.

Not the lower case, muttered behind my back kind or the seemingly harmless 'chubby' or 'cuddly'. I'm not even the more sophisticated 'voluptuous' or 'curvaceous' kind. Let's not sugar coat it, I am the capital F.A.T. kind of FAT. I am the elephant in the room.

When I walked out on stage, maybe some of you thought, 'Oh this is going to be hilarious 'cos everybody knows fat people are funny.' Or maybe you thought, 'Where does she get her confidence from?' because a confident fat woman is almost unthinkable. The fashion-conscious members of the audience may have been thinking how fabulous I look in this Beth Ditto dress, while some of you may have thought, 'Hmmm, black would have been so much more slimming.'

You may have wondered – consciously or not – if I have diabetes, or a partner, or if I eat carbs after 7 p.m. Maybe you started to worry that YOU ate carbs after 7 p.m. last night, and that you really should renew your gym membership. These judgments are insidious. They can be directed at individuals or groups and they can also be directed at ourselves. And this way of thinking is known as fat-phobia.

Like any form of systematic oppression, fat-phobia is deeply rooted in complex structures like capitalism, patriarchy and racism. And that can make it difficult to see, let alone challenge. We live in a culture where being fat is associated with being a bad person – lazy, greedy, unhealthy, irresponsible and morally suspect. And we tend to see thinness as universally good – disciplined, successful, and in control of our appetites, bodies and lives. We see these ideas again and again in the media, in public health policy, doctors' offices, everyday conversations and in our own attitudes.

We may even blame fat people themselves for the discrimination they face. Because after all, if we don't like it, we should just lose weight ... Easy! This anti-fat bias has become so ingrained, so integral to how we value ourselves and each other, that we rarely question why we have such contempt for people of size or where that disdain comes from. But we MUST question it – because the enormous value we place on how we look affects every one of us. And do we really want to live in a world where people are denied their basic humanity if they don't conform to an arbitrary standard of 'acceptable'?

When I was six years old, my sister used to teach ballet to a bunch of little girls in our garage. I was about a foot taller and a foot wider than most of the group.

When it came to doing our first show, I was so excited about wearing a pretty pink tutu. I was going to SPARKLE! As the other girls slipped easily into their lycra and tulle creations, not one of the tutus was big enough to fit me. I was determined not to be excluded from the performance. I turned to my mother and, loud enough for everyone to hear, triumphantly said, 'Mum, I don't need a tutu, I need … A FourFour'. And although I didn't realise it at the time, claiming space for myself in my glorious FourFour was the first step towards becoming a radical fat activist.

Now, I'm not saying that this whole body love thing has been an easy skip along a glittering path of self-acceptance since that day in class. Far from it. I soon learnt that living outside what the mainstream considers 'normal' can be a frustrating and isolating place. I've spent the last 20 years unpacking and deprogramming these messages, and it's been quite the rollercoaster. I have been openly laughed at, abused from passing cars and accused of being delusional. I also get smiles from strangers who recognise what it takes to walk down the street with a spring in your step and your head held high. But through it all that fierce little six-year-old has stayed with me. And she has helped me to stand before you today as an unapologetic fat person. A person that simply refuses to subscribe to the dominant narrative about how I should move through the world in this body of mine. And I am not alone.

I am part of an international community of people who don't just passively accept that our bodies are and probably always will be big, but rather who actively choose to flourish in our bodies as they are today.

People who honour our strength, and work with, not against, our perceived limitations. People who view health as something much more holistic than a number on a BMI chart. Instead, we value mental health, self-worth and how we feel in our bodies as vital aspects of our overall well-being. People who reject the idea that living in these fat bodies is a barrier to, well, anything really.

There are doctors, academics and bloggers who have written countless volumes on the many facets of this complex subject. There are fatshionistas who reclaim their bodies and their beauty by wearing fatkinis and crop tops exposing the flesh we are all taught to hide. There are fat athletes who run marathons, teach yoga or do kickboxing. All done with a middle finger firmly held up to the status quo. This community has taught me that Radical Body Politics is the antidote to our body shaming culture.

To be clear, I am not saying that people shouldn't change their bodies if they want to. Transforming yourself can be the most radical act of self-love and it can look like a million different things. From hairstyles to tattoos, to body contouring, to hormones and surgery. And yes, even weight loss. It's simple. You decide what is best for your own body. So my way of engaging in activism is by doing all the things that we fatties aren't supposed to do, encouraging other people to join me, then making art about it.

The common thread through most of this work has been reclaiming spaces that are prohibitive to bigger bodies – from the catwalk to club shows, from public swimming pools to prominent dance stages. And reclaiming space en masse is a not only a powerful artistic statement but a radical community-building approach.

This was so true of Aquaporko! The fat femme synchronised swim team I started with a group of friends in Sydney. The impact of seeing a bunch of defiant fat women in flowery swimming caps and bathers throwing their legs in the air without a care should not to be underestimated. Throughout my career, I have learnt that fat bodies are inherently political, and unapologetic fat bodies can Blow People's Minds!

When director Kate Champion of acclaimed dance theatre company Force Majeure asked me to be the Artistic Associate on a work featuring all fat dancers, I literally jumped at the opportunity. *Nothing to Lose* is a show made in collaboration with performers of size, who drew from their lived experiences to create a work as authentic and varied as we all are. And it was as far from ballet as you can imagine. The very idea of a fat dance work by such a prestigious company was, to put it mildly, controversial.

Because nothing like it had ever been shown on mainstream dance stages before, anywhere in the world.

People were sceptical. 'What do you mean by fat dancers?' 'Like size 10? Size 12 kinda fat?' 'Where did they train?' 'Will they have the stamina for a full-length production?' But despite the scepticism, *Nothing to Lose* became a sell-out hit of Sydney Festival. We received rave reviews, toured, won awards and were written about in over 27 languages. I've lost count of how many times people of all sizes have told me the show has changed their lives. How it has shifted their relationship to their own and other people's bodies. How it made them confront their own bias. But of course, work that pushes people's buttons is not without its detractors.

I've been told that I am glorifying obesity. I have received violent death threats and abuse for daring to make work that centres fat people's bodies and lives, and treats us as worthwhile human beings with valuable stories to tell. I've even been called 'The Isis of the Obesity Epidemic' – a comment so absurd that it's almost funny. But it also shows the panic, the literal terror, the fear that fat can evoke. It is this fear that is feeding the diet culture that is keeping so many of us from making peace with our own bodies. For waiting to be the after photo before we truly start to live our lives. Because the real elephant in the room here is fat-phobia.

Fat Activism refuses to indulge this fear. By advocating for self-determination and respect for all of us we can start to shift society's reluctance to embrace diversity and start to celebrate the myriad of ways there are to have a body.

CHAPTER 3
LOVE

'I fall in love with myself.
And I want someone to share it
with me.
I want someone to share me, with me.'
Eartha Kitt

New Year before last my mates Gloria, Grace and I spent an entire five-hour sweaty taxi ride across a good proportion of Nicaragua talking about our tragic love lives. We analysed dating app prick after dating app prick, compared notes on how to handle finding out you're on a date with a racist, and by the end of the journey we had all deleted Tinder and vowed to be more TENDER. Love seems more complicated and hard to find than ever, and it's easy to become hardened and cynical.

From 2020 primary and secondary schools will be obliged to teach children about relationships, online safety and mental health, which will help with the basics. But throughout history love has troubled artists, writers, philosophers and *Love Island* contestants – why do we expect ourselves to know what the heck it's all about?

Women from history empathise with our troubles. The 16th-century enigma Jane Anger recounts troubles with men that will be reminiscent of many a troubled Tinder swiper. The forever single Mary Astell of the same period questions why anyone would imagine they could have a happy marriage.

One of the most famous, beloved monologues of actors, Rose's speech from *Fences*, painfully expresses the heartache of being taken for granted in a loveless relationship, fighting for your partner to see you and your struggle. Then there are those of us who have had to fight to love at all. Beverley Ditsie was the first African lesbian to address the UN about the right to love other women. Whatever you're going through, there are centuries of women who see you.

But we start with perhaps the most famous wife in the world, Michelle Obama, at the beginning of her political journey from breadwinner to First Lady and who knows what next? President?!

MICHELLE OBAMA
(1964–)
THE GUY WHO LIVES AT MY HOUSE

You probably already know quite a bit about Michelle Obama. She grew up in the South Side of Chicago, and was so clever she skipped second grade. She went on to gain places at two of the top universities in the US, Princeton and then Harvard, and became a lawyer at Sidley Austin LLP. That's where, in 1989, she met Barack.

By 2007 she was the breadwinner, with a $273k job at University of Chicago Hospitals. But Barack announced his candidacy for the presidency and things would never be the same. Here, Michelle Obama is giving a speech right at the beginning of that campaign, in New Hampshire, 2007, a campaign that would lead them both to the White House, and make her the first African American First Lady.

This journey that we've been on is just still amazing to me. I am still overwhelmed by it. In fact, I tease Barack all the time when we go to places and somebody says, 'there's a thousand people in there to see you,' and I think well *who* are they there to see? Is it Bruce Springsteen or somebody else? Because I'm still trying to reconcile these two images of Barack Obama: there's Barack Obama the phenomenon and then there's the guy who lives at my house.

And that guy's not so impressive. He still doesn't make his bed any better than our five-year-old. He can't quite get his socks in the dirty clothes. So I tell women he's a wonderful man. He's a phenomenal man. But in the end, he's still a man.

But in all seriousness, I am so proud of my husband and I'm excited that he's made the decision to run for president of the United States. That still amazes me.

And although this is my first trip here to New Hampshire, it won't be the last. One of the roles I think that I can play is not just a surrogate campaigner or messenger, but really as a surrogate ear.

Since this is the first time you all have had the opportunity to meet me, I'm going to spend just a little bit of time telling you about me.

I want to share with you how I was brought up – my upbringing, my values, the sort of things that keep Barack and I grounded – as a way of giving you a sense of how we're going to approach this campaign and how we're going to keep ourselves centred, and how we operate in our lives.

My background is pretty humble. I grew up on the South Side of Chicago in a working-class community. A predominantly African-American community. My father was a city worker, a blue-collar worker, all of his life. He died a year before I got married.

My mother was a stay-at-home mum until I went to high school, and I'm the youngest of two. I've got an older brother. My big brother, who I love dearly, Craig, who is now a basketball coach at Brown University and just moved to the east coast, had a great season this year. Yay! Go Bears!

We are both products of the Chicago public school system. I went to the public schools my entire career. My brother left when he went to high school because he was a scholar athlete, and my parents wanted to make sure he was going to get a good education.

That strategy paid off because he got good grades, and played ball, and earned admission to Princeton University. That was really the first time in my life that I had known somebody who actually got into an Ivy League school. My parents didn't go to college. We had some relatives who had gone to good schools, but that was the first time in my life that I had been exposed to the notion that we could possibly compete and get into a selective Ivy League school.

So when he got in, I thought, well I'm smarter than that guy. So, I applied and I got in as well.

You know, a lot of people ask my brother and I, 'Wow, how did two working-class kids wind up at Princeton University?' And for me, what's *not* so remarkable is the fact that we actually got in and thrived, but what I really think about is how my parents managed it all.

How did they afford to send two kids to Princeton? We were there for two years at the same time. I know that they made a great deal of sacrifice, and now looking back, I know just how much they must have sacrificed to make sure that we could achieve our dreams.

When I think about what has shaped me most, it's really my parents. And they're not extraordinary people. They are very ordinary hard-working people. But my father, in particular, touches me and my brother the most.

He had multiple sclerosis. He died the year before I got married. For those of you who know anything about MS, it's a degenerative disease and it strikes unexpectedly. My father went from a vibrant athlete in his 20s, served in the military, to not being able to walk or ever run again. He needed the assistance of a stick, and eventually he had to get around on a motorised car.

When I think about my dad, I think about the fact that he never complained once. He never talked about his struggle or his pain. He was never late. He went to work every day. He worked hard. He put every ounce of his energy into taking care of our family.

And what my brother and I learned from our parents, from my father in particular, was perseverance. We learned consistency. We learned the value of hard work. We learned the value of money. We learned that there's nothing more important than family and community.

And when I think about what really guides me in my life, it's that voice in my head that is my father. And I'm always thinking throughout my life, would this make my father proud? Would he think that I'm living my life to the fullest? Am I making the most of the blessings I've received?

JANE ANGER

(Unknown 16th Century)

PROTECTION FOR WOMEN

The fact that the advice from a little-known pamphlet from 1589 could be applied to the dating apps of today is testament to how little ever really changes. While I was researching this first ever published defence of women (in English), I was WhatsApping advice back to a mate currently grappling with a catfish. Jane Anger had obviously come across her fair share.

The problem is no one knows who Anger actually is. Some think she was actually a man, as it is so unlikely that a woman would find herself in the position where she had her writing published. But, I'm going assume Jane Anger was a woman, a pissed-off woman with the perfect surname. And I'm including her here, because even though this is not a speech, it is an incredible achievement to have a pamphlet published at a time where few records of women's thoughts exist, and for us to still be able to read that pamphlet. To me, this is record of a lone voice representing her sex, calling through history to say, Women of 2020 – us in 1589, we feel you.

She begins by reminding us that we shouldn't condemn all men, #notallmen, and goes on to describe the tactics of 'untrue meaning men' who bear a close resemblance to 21st-century anti-feminist f*ck boys.

I have set down unto you (which are of mine owne Sex) the subtil dealings of untrue meaning men: not that you should contemne al men, but to the end that you may take heed of the false hearts of al, & stil reproove the flattery which remaines in all: for as it is reason that the Hennes should be served first, which both lay the egs, & hatch the chickins: so it were unreasonable that the cockes which tread them, should be kept clean without meat.

As men are valiant, so are they vertuous: and those that are borne honorably, cannot beare horrible dissembling heartes. But as there are some which cannot love hartely, so there are many who lust uncessantly, & as many of them wil deserve wel, so most care not how il they spæd so they may get our company. Wherin they resemble Envie, who will be contented to loose one of his eies that another might have both his pulled out. And therefore thinke well of as many as you may, love them that you have cause, heare every thing that they say, (& affoord them noddes which make themselves noddies) but beleeve very little therof or nothing at all, and hate all those, who shall speake any thing in the dispraise or to the dishonor of our sex.

At the end of mens faire promises there is a Laberinth, & therefore ever hereafter stoppe your eares when they protest friendship, lest they come to an end before you are aware wherby you fal without redemption. The path which leadeth therunto, is Mans wit, and the miles ends are marked with these trees, Follie, Vice, Mischiefe, Lust, Deceite, & Pride. These to deceive you shall bee clothed in the raimentes of Fancie, Vertue, Modestie, Love, Truemeaning, and Handsomnes. Folly wil bid you welcome on your way, & tel you his fancie, concerning the profite which may come to you by this jorney, and direct you to Vice who is more craftie.

He with a company of protestations will praise the vertues of women, shewing how many waies men are beholden unto us: but our backes once turned, he fals a railing.

Then Mischiefe he pries into every corner of us, seeing if he can espy a cranny, that getting in his finger into it, he may make it wide enough for his tong to wag in. Now being come to Lust: he will fall a railing on lascivious lookes, & wil ban Lecherie, & with the Collier will say, the devill take him though he never means it. Deceit will geve you faire words, & pick your pockets: nay he will pluck out your hearts, if you be not wary. But when you heare one cry out against lawnes, drawn-workes, Periwigs, against the attire of Curtizans, & generally of the pride of al women: then know him for a Wolfe clothed in sheepes raiment, and be sure you are fast by the lake of destruction.

Therfore take heed of it, which you shall doe, if you shun mens flattery, the forerunner of our undoing. If a jade be galled, wil he not winch? and can you finde fault with a horse that springeth when he is spurred? The one will stand quietly when his backe is healed, and the other go wel when his smart ceaseth. You must beare with the olde Lover his surfeit, because hee was diseased when he did write it, and peradventure hereafter, when he shal be well amended, he wil repent himselfe of his slanderous speaches against our sex, and curse the dead man which was the cause of it, and make a publique recantation: For the faltering in his speach at the latter end of his book affirmeth, that already he half repenteth of his bargaine, & why? because his melodie is past: but beleeve him not, thogh he shold out swear you, for althogh a jade may be still in a stable when his gall backe is healed, yet hee will showe himselfe in his kind when he is travelling: and mans flattery bites secretly, from which I pray God keepe you and me too.

MARY ASTELL

(1666–1731)

REFLECTIONS UPON MARRIAGE

We definitely know who Mary Astell is, because she is known as the first English feminist. She was a writer and debater, and part of a squad of 17th-century literary women in Chelsea who helped her get her work published. *Reflections Upon Marriage* is one of those works, and I'm including this written text in a book of speeches because without record of her debate speeches, we must assume that if she wrote it, she would have said it.

Astell engaged in philosophical debates with women and men, proposing that women too had the ability to reason, and is quoted as having said, 'If all Men are born Free, why are all Women born Slaves?' Yet, even with this uncompromising analysis of the uneven, abusive power dynamic between men and women, you'll see that Astell calls women to look for friendship with a man in marriage. Perhaps this was just a survival strategy in a relationship she saw as fundamentally unfair, and where women were treated like property: you were judged on how many acres came with you in the marriage deal.

And did Astell marry?

NO.

But if Marriage be such a blessed State, how comes it, may you say, that there are so few happy Marriages?

Now in answer to this, it is not to be wonder'd that so few succeed, we should rather be surpriz'd to find so many do, considering how imprudently Men engage, the Motives they act by, and the very strange Conduct they observe throughout.

For pray, what do Men propose to themselves in Marriage? What Qualifications do they look after in a Spouse? What will she bring is the first enquiry? How many Acres? Or how much ready Coin? Not that this is altogether an unnecessary Question, for Marriage without a Competency, that is, not only a bare Subsistence, but even a handsome and plentiful Provision, according to the Quality and Circumstances of the Parties, is no very comfortable Condition.

They who Marry for Love as they call it, find time enough to repent their rash Folly, and are not long in being convinc'd, that whatever fine Speeches might be made in the heat of Passion, there could be no real Kindness between those who can agree to make each other miserable.

But as an estate is to be consider'd, so it should not be the Main, much less the Only consideration, for Happiness does not depend on Wealth, that may be wanting, and too often is, where this abounds. He who Marries himself to a Fortune only, must expect no other satisfaction than that can bring him, but let him not say that Marriage but that his own Covetous or Prodigal Temper, has made him unhappy.

It is even so in the Case before us; a Woman who has been taught to think Marriage her only Preferment, the sum-total of her Endeavours, the completion of all her hopes, that which must settle and make her Happy in this World, and very few, in their Youth especially, carry a Thought steddily to a greater distance; She who has seen a Lover dying at her Feet, and can't therefore imagine that he who professes to receive all his Happiness from her can have any other Design or Desire than to please her; whose Eyes have been dazled with all the Glitter and Pomp of a Wedding, and who hears of nothing but Joy and Congratulation; who is transported with the Pleasure of being out of Pupillage and Mistress not only of her self but of a Family too: She who is either so simple or so vain, as to take her Lover at his Word either as to the Praises he gave her, or the Promises he made for himself: In sum, she whose Expectation has been rais'd by Court-ship, by all the fine things that her Lover, her Governess and Domestick Flatterers say, will find a terrible disappointment when the hurry is over, and when she comes calmly to consider her Condition, and views it no more under a false Appearance, but as it truly is.

BEVERLEY (BEV) PALESA DITSIE

(1971-)

UN ADDRESS

Another First Lady of history – Ditsie was the first out African lesbian to address the UN on LGBT rights in 1995 with this speech at the UN 4th Conference on Women.

It was the height of Apartheid when Ditsie was born in Soweto. She grew up to be a high-profile anti-Apartheid and LGBT activist, with support from Nelson Mandela, and was one of the founders of Pride in South Africa. Ditsie took the most personal of human behaviours – love, sex, relationships – and bravely fought for the right to love whoever you want, and the protection of that right. She didn't have to. She could have stayed at home and kept her love secret. However, she made the personal political, global, and changed the world.

Madam Chair,

It is a great honour to have the opportunity to address this distinguished body on behalf of the International Gay and Lesbian Human Rights Commission, the International Lesbian Information Service, the International Lesbian and Gay Association and over 50 other organisations. My name is Palesa Beverley Ditsie and I am from Soweto, South Africa, where I have lived all my life and experienced both tremendous joy and pain within my community. I come from a country that has recently had an opportunity to start afresh, an opportunity to strive for a true democracy where the people govern and where emphasis is placed on the human rights of all people. The Constitution of South Africa prohibits discrimination on the basis of race, gender, ethnic or social origin, colour, sexual orientation, age, disability, religion, conscience, belief, culture or language. In his opening parliamentary speech in Cape Town on 9th April 1994, His Excellency Nelson Rolihlahla Mandela, State President of South Africa, received resounding applause when he declared that never again would anyone be discriminated against on the basis of sexual orientation.

The Universal Declaration of Human Rights recognises the 'inherent dignity and ... the equal and inalienable rights of all members of the human family', and guarantees the protection of the fundamental rights and freedoms of all people 'without distinction of any kind, such as race, colour, sex, language ... or other status' (art. 2). Yet every day, in countries around the world, lesbians suffer violence, harassment and discrimination because of their sexual orientation. Their basic human rights – such as the right to life, to bodily integrity, to freedom of association and expression – are violated. Women who love women are fired from their jobs; forced into marriages; beaten and murdered in their homes and on the streets; and have their children taken away by hostile courts. Some commit suicide due to the isolation and stigma that they experience within their families, religious institutions and their broader community. These and other abuses are documented in a recently released report by the International Gay and Lesbian Human Rights Commission on sexual orientation and women's human rights, as well as in reports by Amnesty International. Yet the majority of these abuses have been difficult to document because although lesbians exist everywhere in the world (including Africa), we have been marginalised and silenced and remain invisible in most of the world. In 1994, the United Nations Human Rights Committee declared that discrimination based on sexual orientation violates the right to non-discrimination and the right to privacy guaranteed in the International Covenant of Civil and Political Rights. Several countries have passed legislation prohibiting discrimination based on sexual orientation. If the World Conference on Women is to address the concerns of all women, it must similarly recognise that discrimination based on sexual orientation is a violation of basic human rights. Paragraphs 48 and 226 of the Platform for Action recognise that women face particular barriers in their lives because of many factors, including sexual orientation. However, the term 'sexual orientation' is currently in brackets. If these words are omitted from the relevant paragraphs, the Platform for Action will stand as one more symbol of the discrimination that lesbians face, and of the lack of recognition of our very existence.

No woman can determine the direction of her own life without the ability to determine her sexuality. Sexuality is an integral, deeply ingrained part of every human being's life and should not be subject to debate or coercion. Anyone who is truly committed to women's human rights must recognise that every woman has the right to determine her sexuality free of discrimination and oppression.

I urge you to make this a conference for all women, regardless of their sexual orientation, and to recognise in the Platform for Action that lesbian rights are women's rights and that women's rights are universal, inalienable and indivisible human rights. I urge you to remove the brackets from sexual orientation.

Thank you.

ROSE MAXSON

(1985)

ROSE'S MONOLOGUE FROM 'FENCES' (Play by August Wilson)

From the authentic voice of an African woman who stood up to the world, to the iconic words of an African-American character – Rose – who stands up to her husband in male playwright August Wilson's 1985 play *Fences*. It's won the Pulitzer Prize and Tony Awards. Viola Davis won Best Supporting Actress at the Oscars in 2017 for her portrayal of Rose.

It's a bit of a controversial move putting words we definitely know are a man's in a book of speeches by women. Men have written, painted, played the representation of women through the centuries, and this book is about celebrating women's words. However, this speech transgresses the normal boundaries of who owns these words.

Rose's monologue is one of the most popular women's monologues. Women across the world choose it for auditions, theatre exams and just for the pleasure of spitting it out, expressing it. And I'm arguing by including it that this speech isn't August's, it's every woman's who plays Rose and who brings her emotions and memories to the role.

Who doesn't recognise the pain in Rose here? In Rose's 1950s world devoting yourself to an, at best, apathetic, at worst, abusive, partner was a means of survival, and the fulfilment of what you were taught was the right and proper thing to do. My guess is that this speech resonates so much because it's an explosion of truth for generations of women. We need to say these words.

I been standing with you! I been right here with you, Troy. I got a life too. I gave 18 years of my life to stand in the same spot with you.

Don't you think I ever wanted other things? Don't you think I had dreams and hopes? What about my life? What about me? Don't you think it ever crossed my mind to want to know other men?

That I wanted to lay up somewhere and forget about my responsibilities? That I wanted someone to make me laugh so I could feel good? You not the only one who's got wants and needs. But I held on to you, Troy. I took all my feelings, my wants and needs, my dreams ... and I buried them inside you. I planted a seed and watched and prayed over it. I planted myself inside you and waited to bloom. And it didn't take me no 18 years to find out the soil was hard and rocky and it wasn't never gonna bloom.

But I held on to you, Troy. I held you tighter. You was my husband. I owed you everything I had. Every part of

me I could find to give you. And upstairs in that room ...
with the darkness falling in on me ... I gave everything I
had to try and erase the doubt that you wasn't the finest
man in the world. And wherever you was going ... I wanted
to be there with you. 'Cause you was my husband. 'Cause
that's the only way I was gonna survive as your wife. You
always talking about what you give ... and what you don't
have to give. But you take, too. You take ... and don't even
know nobody's giving!

CHAPTER 4

BOYS WILL BE ... ALLIES

'If my male co-star, who has a higher quote than me but believes we are equal, takes a pay cut so that I can match him, that changes my quote in the future and changes my life.'
Emma Stone

In the late noughties, spurred on by sexism at gigs, I started a punk feminist choir. No men. For the first few years I was determined that we would only work with women. Our lawyer was a woman. Our manager was a woman. We self-ghettoised. And it was brilliant, it worked, it meant we broke through the noise and were seen and heard. But, ghettoisation isn't the way to get lasting change; everyone working together is the way.

Women need men to share, in order for there to be long-term change. We need them to willingly share power, money and space with us. It's a hard sell, which is why we need to do the same. White women need to share with women of colour. Cis women need to share with trans women. Third-generation immigrants need to share with first-generation. It doesn't mean each group can't have its own protections and spaces (I'd definitely encourge men to have their own space). But, in the same way Emma Stone's colleagues need to cut their wage in order for her to be paid the same, we need to challenge ourselves and others to act in solidarity with those who are fighting for equality.

Andrea Dworkin challenged 500 men to organise a 24-hour rape truce, saying that there could be no equality until they did. Huda Sha'arwiri confronted the first Arab Feminist Conference with the message that men had divvied up the power in their own favour and women had not signed off on the arrangement. Australian Prime Minister, Julia Gillard still had to battle her male peers into giving her the respect she was due. Emma Watson launched the UN HeForShe campaign by explaining feminism is not man-hating, and urged us to get men and boys on side to finally make the world fair for women and girls.

These women inspired men and women into partnering on equality.

ANDREA DWORKIN

(1946-2005)

24-HOUR RAPE TRUCE

Dworkin was a radical American feminist writer and activist. She was to the media the embodiment of the monster, man-hating feminist. So much so she was cast as the feminist that inspired the backlash against feminism.

She was in fact a softly-spoken campaigner, twice married to men, who suffered abuse throughout her life and career, and tirelessly fought for the rights of women. Her work was, and continues to be, controversial, with many liberal feminists considering her an extremist. But, whether you agree or strongly disagree with her, she is a very important figure in feminist history.

This is an extract from a speech she gave at the Midwest Regional Conference of the National Organization for Changing Men in 1983 in St Paul, Minnesota, to about 500 men. What would you say to 500 men if you had the opportunity?

I have thought a great deal about how a feminist, like myself, addresses an audience primarily of political men who say that they are antisexist. And I thought a lot about whether there should be a qualitative difference in the kind of speech I address to you. And then I found myself incapable of pretending that I really believe that qualitative difference exists. I have watched the men's movement for many years. I am close with some of the people who participate in it. I can't come here as a friend even though I might very much want to. What I would like to do is to scream: and in that scream I would have the screams of the raped, and the sobs of the battered; and even worse, in the centre of that scream I would have the deafening sound of women's silence, that silence into which we are born because we are women and in which most of us die.

And if there would be a plea or a question or a human address in that scream, it would be this: why are you so slow? Why are you so slow to understand the simplest things; not the complicated ideological things. You understand those. The simple things. The clichés. Simply that women are human to precisely the degree and quality that you are.

And also: that we do not have time. We women. We don't have forever. Some of us don't have another week or another day to take time for you to discuss whatever it is that will enable you to go out into those streets and do something. We are very close to death. All women are. And we are very close to rape and we are very close to beating. And we are inside a system of humiliation from which there is no escape for us. We use statistics not to try to quantify the injuries, but to convince the world that those injuries even exist. Those statistics are not abstractions. It is easy to say, 'Ah, the statistics, somebody writes them up one way and somebody writes them up another way.' That's true. But I hear about the rapes one by one by one by one by one, which is also how they happen. Those statistics are not abstract to me. Every three minutes a woman is being raped. Every eighteen seconds a woman is being beaten. There is nothing abstract about it. It is happening right now as I am speaking.

I want to see this men's movement make a commitment to ending rape because that is the only meaningful commitment to equality. It is astonishing that in all our worlds of feminism and antisexism we never talk seriously about ending rape. Ending it. Stopping it. No more. No more rape. In the back of our minds, are we holding on to its inevitability as the last preserve of the biological? Do we think that it is always going to exist no matter what we do? All of our political actions are lies if we don't make a commitment to ending the practice of rape. This commitment has to be political. It has to be serious. It has to be systematic. It has to be public. It can't be self-indulgent.

The things the men's movement has wanted are things worth having. Intimacy is worth having. Tenderness is worth having. Co-operation is worth having. A real emotional life is worth having. But you can't have them in a world with rape. Ending homophobia is worth doing. But you can't do it in a world with rape. Rape stands in the way of each and every one of those things you say you want. And by rape you know what I mean. A judge does not have to walk into this room and say that according to statute such and such these are the elements of proof. We're talking about any kind of coerced sex, including sex coerced by poverty.

You can't have equality or tenderness or intimacy as long as there is rape, because rape means terror. It means that part of the population lives in a state of terror and pretends – to please and pacify you – that it doesn't. So there is no honesty. How can there be?

Have you ever wondered why we are not just in armed combat against you? It's not because there's a shortage of kitchen knives in this country. It is because we believe in your humanity, against all the evidence.

As a feminist, I carry the rape of all the women I've talked to over the last ten years personally with me. As a woman, I carry my own rape with me. Do you remember pictures that you've seen of European cities during the plague, when there were wheelbarrows that would go along and people would just pick up corpses and throw them in? Well, that is what it is like knowing about rape. Piles and piles and piles of bodies that have whole lives and human names and human faces.

I speak for many feminists, not only myself, when I tell you that I am tired of what I know and sad beyond any words I have about what has already been done to women up to this point, now, here in this place.

And I want one day of respite, one day off, one day in which no new bodies are piled up, one day in which no new agony is added to the old, and I am asking you to give it to me. And how could I ask you for less – it is so little. And how could you offer me less – it is so little. Even in wars, there are days of truce. Go and organise a truce. Stop your side for one day. I want a 24-hour truce during which there is no rape.

And on that day, that day of truce, that day when not one woman is raped, we will begin the real practice of equality, because we can't begin it before that day. Before that day it means nothing because it is nothing: it is not real; it is not true. But on that day it becomes real. And then, instead of rape we will for the first time in our lives – both men and women – begin to experience freedom.

If you have a conception of freedom that includes the existence of rape, you are wrong. You cannot change what you say you want to change. For myself, I want to experience just one day of real freedom before I die. I leave you here to do that for me and for the women whom you say you love.

HUDA (HODA) SHA'ARAWI

(1879–1947)

OPENING SPEECH TO THE FIRST ARAB FEMINIST CONFERENCE, CAIRO, 1944

Sha'arawi was also a radical. She didn't just lead a feminist movement in Egypt, she led protests against British rule. She removed her veil publicly and rejected the harem system, which she had grown up in and which separated women and men.

The Egyptian Feminist Union was founded in her home on the 6th March 1923, and she fought for education for women and girls, and to free women's socio-economic status. In her opening speech to the first Arab Feminist Conference she made a rallying cry to men, demanding they empathise with women's oppression, as they too had been oppressed by the colonial power.

Ladies and Gentlemen, the Arab woman who is equal to the man in duties and obligations will not accept, in the 20th century, the distinctions between the sexes that the advanced countries have done away with. The Arab woman will not agree to be chained in slavery and to pay for the consequences of men's mistakes with respect to her country's rights and the future of her children. The woman also demands with her loudest voice to be restored her political rights, rights granted to her by the Sharia and dictated to her by the demands of the present. The advanced nations have recognised that the man and the woman are to each other like the brain and heart are to the body; if the balance between these two organs is upset, the system of the whole body will be upset. Likewise, if the balance between the two sexes in the nation is upset it will disintegrate and collapse. The advanced nations, after careful examination into the matter, have come to believe in the equality of sexes in all rights even though their religious and secular laws have not reached the level Islam has reached in terms of justice to the woman.

Islam has given her the right to vote for the ruler and has allowed her to give opinions on questions of jurisprudence and religion. The woman, given by the Creator the right to vote for the successor of the Prophet, is deprived of the right to vote for a deputy in a circuit or district election by a (male) being created by God. At the same time, this right is enjoyed by a man who might have less education and experience than the woman. And she is the mother who has given birth to the man and has raised and guided him. The Sharia gave her the right to education, to take part in the *hijra* and to fight in the ranks of warriors, and has made her the equal to the man in all rights and responsibilities, even in the crimes that either sex can commit.

However, the man, who alone distributes rights, has kept for himself the right to legislate and rule, generously turning over to his partner his own share of responsibilities and sanctions without seeking her opinion about the division. The woman today demands to regain her share of rights that have been taken from her and gives back to the man the responsibilities and sanctions he has given to her.

Gentlemen, this is justice, and I do not believe that the Arab man who demands that others give him back his usurped rights would be avaricious and not give the woman back her own lawful rights, all the more so since he himself has tasted the bitterness of deprivation and usurped rights.

JULIA GILLARD AC

(1961–)

MISOGYNY

In a land far away, both geographically and, by 2012, when this speech was given, completely alien in the opportunities women could take advantage of, Gillard had risen to the most powerful position in Australia. However, she was still having to do battle with the men she counted as her peers.

Gillard was the first woman to be Australia's Prime Minister. Originally from Barry in Wales, she migrated in 1966. She was a lawyer before moving into politics. In this speech she took offence at the opposition, Tony Abbott's, motion to remove Peter Slipper as Speaker, because of some inappropriate texts, which Abbott characterised as sexist. He went on to describe every day of Gillard's support for Slipper as 'another day of shame for a government which should already have died of shame'.

After the speech went viral Macquarie Dictionary changed the definition of misogyny from 'hatred of women', to include 'entrenched prejudice against women'. Here Julia Gillard explains why she will not be lectured by Abbott on misogyny.

Thank you very much, Deputy Speaker, and I rise to oppose the motion moved by the Leader of the Opposition. And in so doing I say to the Leader of the Opposition I will not be lectured about sexism and misogyny by this man. I will not. And the Government will not be lectured about sexism and misogyny by this man. Not now, not ever.

The Leader of the Opposition says that people who hold sexist views and who are misogynists are not appropriate for high office. Well, I hope the Leader of the Opposition has got a piece of paper and he is writing out his resignation. Because if he wants to know what misogyny looks like in modern Australia, he doesn't need a motion in the House of Representatives, he needs a mirror. That's what he needs.

Let's go through the Opposition Leader's repulsive double standards, repulsive double standards when it comes to misogyny and sexism. We are now supposed to take seriously that the Leader of the Opposition is offended by Mr Slipper's text messages, when this is the Leader of the Opposition who has said, and this was when he was a minister under the last government – not when he was a student, not when he was in high school – when he was a minister under the last government.

He has said, and I quote, in a discussion about women being under-represented in institutions of power in Australia ... the interviewer was a man called Stavros. The Leader of the Opposition says, 'If it's true, Stavros, that men have more power generally speaking than women, is that a bad thing?'

And then a discussion ensues, and another person says, 'I want my daughter to have as much opportunity as my son.' To which the Leader of the Opposition says, 'Yeah, I completely agree, but what if men are by physiology or temperament more adapted to exercise authority or to issue command?'

Then ensues another discussion about women's role in modern society, and the other person participating in the discussion says, 'I think it's very hard to deny that there is an under-representation of women', to which the Leader of the Opposition says, 'But now, there's an assumption that this is a bad thing.'

This is the man from whom we're supposed to take lectures about sexism. And then of course it goes on. I was very offended personally when the Leader of the Opposition, as Minister of Health, said, and I quote, 'Abortion is the easy way out.' I was very personally offended by those comments. You said that in March 2004, I suggest you check the records.

I was also very offended on behalf of the women of Australia when in the course of this carbon pricing campaign, the Leader of the Opposition said, 'What the housewives of Australia need to understand as they do the ironing ...' Thank you for that painting of women's roles in modern Australia.

And then of course, I was offended too by the sexism, by the misogyny of the Leader of the Opposition catcalling across this table at me as I sit here as Prime Minister, 'If the Prime Minister wants to, politically speaking, make an honest woman of herself ...', something that would never have been said to any man sitting in this chair.

I was offended when the Leader of the Opposition went outside in the front of Parliament and stood next to a sign that said 'Ditch the witch.'

I was offended when the Leader of the Opposition stood next to a sign that described me as a man's bitch. I was offended by those things. Misogyny, sexism, every day from this Leader of the Opposition. Every day in every way, across the time the Leader of the Opposition has sat in that chair and I've sat in this chair, that is all we have heard from him.

And now, the Leader of the Opposition wants to be taken seriously, apparently he's woken up after this track record and all of these statements, and he's woken up and he's gone, 'Oh dear, there's this thing called sexism, oh my lords, there's this thing called misogyny. Now who's one of them? Oh, the Speaker must be because that suits my political purpose.'

Doesn't turn a hair about any of his past statements, doesn't walk into this Parliament and apologise to the women of Australia. Doesn't walk into this Parliament and apologise to me for the things that have come out of his mouth. But now seeks to use this as a battering ram against someone else.

Well, this kind of hypocrisy must not be tolerated, which is why this motion from the Leader of the Opposition should not be taken seriously.

On the conduct of Mr Slipper, and on the text messages that are in the public domain, I have seen the press reports of those text messages. I am offended by their content. I am offended by their content because I am always offended by sexism. I am offended by their content because I am always offended by statements that are anti-women.

I am offended by those things in the same way that I have been offended by things that the Leader of the Opposition has said, and no doubt will continue to say in the future. Because if this today was an exhibition of his new feminine side, well, I don't think we've got much to look forward to in terms of changed conduct.

I am offended by those text messages. But I also believe, in terms of this Parliament making a decision about the speakership, that this Parliament should recognise that there is a court case in progress. That the judge has reserved his decision, that having waited for a number of months for the legal matters surrounding Mr Slipper to come to a conclusion, that this Parliament should see that conclusion.

I believe that is the appropriate path forward, and that people will then have an opportunity to make up their minds with the fullest information available to them.

But whenever people make up their minds about those questions, what I won't stand for, what I will never stand for, is the Leader of the Opposition coming into this place and peddling a double standard. Peddling a standard for Mr Slipper he would not set for himself. Peddling a standard for Mr Slipper he has not set for other members of his frontbench.

Peddling a standard for Mr Slipper that has not been acquitted by the people who have been sent out to say the vilest and most revolting things, like his former Shadow Parliamentary Secretary Senator Bernardi.

I will not ever see the Leader of the Opposition seek to impose his double standard on this Parliament. Sexism should always be unacceptable. We should conduct ourselves as it should always be unacceptable. The Leader of the Opposition says do something; well, he could do something himself if he wants to deal with sexism in this Parliament.

He could change his behaviour, he could apologise for all his past statements, he could apologise for standing next to signs describing me as a witch and a bitch, terminology that is now objected to by the frontbench of the Opposition.

He could change a standard himself if he sought to do so. But we will see none of that from the Leader of the Opposition because on these questions he is incapable of change. Capable of double standards, but incapable of change. His double standards should not rule this Parliament.

Good sense, common sense, proper process is what should rule this Parliament. That's what I believe is the path forward for this Parliament, not the kind of double standards and political game-playing imposed by the Leader of the Opposition now looking at his watch because apparently a woman's spoken too long.

EMMA WATSON

(1990–)

HEFORSHE

Two years later, one of the most famous women in the world, Watson, as Goodwill Ambassador, took to the stage to launch the UN HeForShe campaign, a solidarity movement promoting gender equality.

Watson was already a role model to young women the world over having played Hermione in the *Harry Potter* films. This was Watson's first major step into activism and it was sure to turn millions of women and girls onto feminism, by demystifying, even destigmatising feminism.

And, just like Dworkin did decades earlier in her own very different way, Watson passionately conveys that we need men and women to work together to achieve equality.

Today we are launching a campaign called 'HeForShe.'

I am reaching out to you because I need your help. We want to end gender inequality – and to do that we need everyone to be involved.

This is the first campaign of its kind at the UN: we want to try and galvanise as many men and boys as possible to be advocates for gender equality. And we don't just want to talk about it, but make sure it is tangible.

I was appointed six months ago and the more I have spoken about feminism, the more I have realised that fighting for women's rights has too often become synonymous with man-hating. If there is one thing I know for certain, it is that this has to stop.

For the record, feminism by definition is: 'The belief that men and women should have equal rights and opportunities. It is the theory of the political, economic and social equality of the sexes.'

Why is the word such an uncomfortable one?

I am from Britain and think it is right that as a woman I am paid the same as my male counterparts. I think it is right that I should be able to make decisions about my own body. I think it is right that women be involved on my behalf in the policies and decision-making of my country. I think it is right that socially I am afforded the same respect as men. But sadly I can say that there is no one country in the world where all women can expect to receive these rights.

No country in the world can yet say they have achieved gender equality.

These rights I consider to be human rights but I am one of the lucky ones. My life is a sheer privilege because my parents didn't love me less because I was born a daughter. My school did not limit me because I was a girl. My mentors didn't assume I would go less far because I might give birth to a child one day. These influencers were the gender equality ambassadors that made me who I am today. They may not know it, but they are the inadvertent feminists who are changing the world today. And we need more of those.

And if you still hate the word – it is not the word that is important, but the idea and the ambition behind it. Because not all women have been afforded the same rights that I have. In fact, statistically, very few have been.

In 1995, Hillary Clinton made a famous speech in Beijing about women's rights. Sadly many of the things she wanted to change are still a reality today.

But what stood out for me the most was that only 30 of her audience were male. How can we effect change in the world when only half of it is invited or feel welcome to participate in the conversation?

Men – I would like to take this opportunity to extend your formal invitation. Gender equality is your issue too.

Because to date, I've seen my father's role as a parent being valued less by society despite my needing his presence as a child as much as my mother's.

I've seen young men suffering from mental illness unable to ask for help for fear it would make them look less 'macho' – in fact in the UK suicide is the biggest killer of men between 20–49 years of age, eclipsing road accidents, cancer and coronary heart disease. I've seen men made fragile and insecure by a distorted sense of what constitutes male success. Men don't have the benefits of equality either.

We don't often talk about men being imprisoned by gender stereotypes but I can see that they are and that when they are free, things will change for women as a natural consequence.

If men don't have to be aggressive in order to be accepted, women won't feel compelled to be submissive. If men don't have to control, women won't have to be controlled.

Both men and women should feel free to be sensitive. Both men and women should feel free to be strong ... It is time that we all perceive gender on a spectrum, not as two opposing sets of ideals.

If we stop defining each other by what we are not and start defining ourselves by what we are, we can all be freer, and this is what HeForShe is about. It's about freedom.

I want men to take up this mantle. So their daughters, sisters and mothers can be free from prejudice, but also so that their sons have permission to be vulnerable and human too, reclaim those parts of themselves they abandoned and in doing so be a more true and complete version of themselves.

You might be thinking, who is this *Harry Potter* girl? And what is she doing up on stage at the UN? It's a good question and, trust me, I have been asking myself the same thing. I don't know if I am qualified to be here. All I know is that I care about this problem. And I want to make it better.

And having seen what I've seen – and given the chance – I feel it is my duty to say something. English Statesman Edmund Burke said, 'All that is needed for the forces of evil to triumph is for enough good men and women to do nothing.'

In my nervousness for this speech and in my moments of doubt I've told myself firmly – if not me, who, if not now, when? If you have similar doubts when opportunities are presented to you I hope those words might be helpful.

Because the reality is that if we do nothing it will take 75 years, or for me to be nearly a hundred, before women can expect to be paid the same as men for the same work. 15.5 million girls will be married in the next 16 years as children. And at current rates it won't be until 2086 before all rural African girls will be able to receive a secondary education.

If you believe in equality, you might be one of those inadvertent feminists I spoke of earlier.

And for this I applaud you.

We are struggling for a uniting word but the good news is we have a uniting movement. It is called HeForShe. I am inviting you to step forward, to be seen to speak up, to be the 'he' for 'she'. And to ask yourself, if not me, who? If not now, when?

Thank you.

CHAPTER 5

END WHITE SUPREMACY

'As long as women are using class or race power to dominate other women, feminist sisterhood cannot be fully realised.'

bell hooks

We are living in a time where there is a rise in white supremacist terrorism and we have to stop it for good.

I'm white, and I benefit from white privilege. I know that no matter how hard it has felt for me to get a platform and have a voice, I still had the odds more in my favour because of that privilege. Sometimes it's difficult for white women to accept that privilege. After all, there are all kinds of nuances around the privileges people do and don't have. Race, class, mental health, disability, sexuality, trauma, religion, immigration, body or gender nonconformity are all characteristics and experiences that affect a person's experience of power dynamics and oppression.

I'm saying this not because I want to minimise racism, but to say to white working-class women, who are struggling, that acknowledging white privilege doesn't take away from your experience. And it's this misunderstanding that I believe has a part in fuelling the current rise in racism and hate crimes. We shouldn't be fighting each other.

This is exactly why intersectional feminism (a term coined by academic and civil rights activist Kimberlé Williams Crenshaw) is essential. Womanhood is not one type of experience, but there are big similarities and shared foes we can work on and fight together.

So, back to speeches. History has silenced and rewritten women to make them acceptable, and women of colour have suffered immense censorship. But, even if you haven't heard of them they are there! Taking greater risks to be heard in spite of slavery, state-sanctioned institutional racism and white supremacy.

This book has speeches from women across the world. In this chapter I've concentrated on African-American and Black British women. There are many other struggles, but these are familiar ones for the people where this book is published – the UK. What's important is we take the lessons from these stories and apply them to other areas of the world. Through Sojourner Truth, who escaped slavery, we learn how she fought to be considered a woman at all, and even through the documentation of her speech we see how engrained racism shapes history.

Through the child of slaves Mary Bethune, we hear how she and her contemporaries created a vision of true democracy, which through their sacrifice came true – to an extent. Because it is then through the experience of abuse of democratically elected Diane Abbott, we know that we are far from the vision of a world where racism does not exist.

White supremacy is one of the most dangerous forces we face today. We must all fight the othering and dehumanising of immigrants and refugees. That's why I include Jacinda Ardern at the end of this chapter. Her recent speech as New Zealand Prime Minister condemning the terrorist attack on two mosques in Christchurch calls on us all to use our 'power to change'.

And finally, because in this chapter I am just an ally and a signpost to women of colour, I want to recommend Reni Eddo-Lodge's seminal book *Why I'm No Longer Talking To White People About Race* and suggest you follow @Gal-dem on all the socials.

SOJOURNER TRUTH

(1797–1883)

AIN'T I A WOMAN

Truth was born into slavery, but escaped with her daughter. She became the first black woman to win a case against a white man to recover her son. An abolitionist and women's rights activist, Sojourner Truth is famous for having said 'Ain't I A Woman', but things aren't always how they appear and we are going to look at two versions of the same speech, for reasons that will become obvious.

The first version was documented by Frances Gage, a white abolitionist and women's rights activist, who invited Truth to speak at the 1851 Women's Rights Convention, Akron, Ohio, in front of some of the WOKEST people of the 19th century.

The parts written phonetically are Sojourner, and Frances is in bold.

'Wall, chilern, whar dar is so much racket dar must be somethin' out o' kilter. I tink dat 'twixt de niggers of de Souf and de womin at de Norf, all talkin' 'bout rights, de white men will be in a fix pretty soon. But what's all dis here talkin' 'bout?

Dat man ober dar say dat womin needs to be helped into carriages, and lifted ober ditches, and to hab de best place everywhar. Nobody eber helps me into carriages, or ober mud-puddles, or gibs me any best place!' **And raising herself to her full height, and her voice to a pitch like rolling thunder, she asked**, 'And ain't I a woman? Look at me! Look at my arm!' **(and she bared her right arm to the shoulder, showing her tremendous muscular power).** 'I have ploughed, and planted, and gathered into barns, and no man could head me! And ain't I a woman? I could work as much and eat as much as a man – when I could get it – and bear de lash as well! And ain't I a woman? I have borne 13 chilern, and seen 'em mos' all sold off to slavery, and when I cried out with my mother's grief, none but Jesus heard me! And ain't I a woman?

Den dey talks 'bout dis ting in de head; what dis dey call it?' ('Intellect,' whispered someone near.) 'Dat's it, honey. What's dat got to do wid womin's rights or nigger's rights? If my cup won't hold but a pint, and yourn holds a quart, wouldn't ye be mean not to let me have my little half-measure full?' **And she pointed her significant finger, and sent a keen glance at the minister who had made the argument. The cheering was long and loud.**

'Den dat little man in back dar, he say women can't have as much rights as men, 'cause Christ wan't a woman! Whar did your Christ come from?' **Rolling thunder couldn't have stilled that crowd, as did those deep, wonderful tones, as she stood there with out-stretched arms and eyes of fire. Raising her voice still louder, she repeated,** 'Whar did your Christ come from? From God and a woman! Man had nothin' to do wid Him.'

Oh, what a rebuke that was to that little man. Turning again to another objector, she took up the defence of Mother Eve. I can not follow her through it all. It was pointed, and witty, and solemn; eliciting at almost every sentence deafening applause; and she ended by asserting:

'If de fust woman God ever made was strong enough to turn de world upside down all alone, dese women togedder' **(and she glanced her eye over the platform)** 'ought to be able to turn it back, and get it right side up again! And now dey is asking to do it, de men better let 'em.' **Long-continued cheering greeted this**. 'Bleeged to ye for hearin' on me, and now ole Sojourner han't got nothin' more to say.'

Amid roars of applause, she returned to her corner leaving more than one of us with streaming eyes, and hearts beating with gratitude. She had taken us up in her strong arms and carried us safely over the slough of difficulty turning the whole tide in our favour. I have never in my life seen anything like the magical influence that subdued the mobbish spirit of the day, and turned the sneers and jeers of an excited crowd into notes of respect and admiration. Hundreds rushed up to shake hands with her, and congratulate the glorious old mother, and bid her God-speed on her mission of 'testifyin' agin concerning the wickedness of this 'ere people'.

In this first version, Gage's voice is ever present, because this was her documentation of the event. This is something we always have to think about when it comes to rhetoric: WHO documented it.

Throughout much of history, it's been a man who has documented a woman's words. Or perhaps even worse: the only documentation we have of the speaker was written by their enemies, for example with Boudicca and Joan of Arc.

Gage cannot help but affect the speech with her own bias, and to put herself very much at the centre of it, no matter how good her intentions may have been ... and this gives us cause for concern. Some people think Gage added the southern dialect, to cast Truth as a caricature and a slave, when Truth would never have had that accent, having lived in New York for most of her life.

So the SECOND version of the speech is a RECLAIMED version. The dialect is gone. Gage is gone. And just Truth's message remains.

AIN'T I A WOMAN RECLAIMED

Well, children, where there is so much racket there must be something out of kilter. I think that 'twixt the negroes of the South and the women at the North, all talking about rights, the white men will be in a fix pretty soon. But what's all this here talking about?

That man over there says that women need to be helped into carriages, and lifted over ditches, and to have the best place everywhere. Nobody ever helps me into carriages, or over mud-puddles, or gives me any best place! And ain't I a woman?

Look at me! Look at my arm! I have ploughed and planted, and gathered into barns, and no man could head me! And ain't I a woman? I could work as much and eat as much as a man – when I could get it – and bear the lash as well! And ain't I a woman? I have borne 13 children, and seen most all sold off to slavery, and when I cried out with my mother's grief, none but Jesus heard me! And ain't I a woman?

Then they talk about this thing in the head; what's this they call it? [member of audience whispers, 'intellect'] That's it, honey. What's that got to do with women's rights or negroes' rights? If my cup won't hold but a pint, and yours holds a quart, wouldn't you be mean not to let me have my little half measure full?

Then that little man in black there, he says women can't have as much rights as men, 'cause Christ wasn't a woman! Where did your Christ come from? Where did your Christ come from? From God and a woman! Man had nothing to do with Him.

If the first woman God ever made was strong enough to turn the world upside down all alone, these women together ought to be able to turn it back, and get it right side up again! And now they is asking to do it, the men better let them.

Obliged to you for hearing me, and now old Sojourner ain't got nothing more to say.

MARY SEACOLE

(1805–1881)

WONDERFUL ADVENTURES OF MRS SEACOLE IN MANY LANDS

Now Mary Seacole made sure no one messed up her story, by writing and getting her own memoirs published. That, however, has not stopped people questioning her account and railing against her becoming a nursing icon.

A British-Jamaican business woman and nurse, Seacole set up a hospital behind the lines of the Crimean War – it was called the British Hotel – and she used all kinds of traditional herbal remedies to nurse soldiers who came to her. While she was famous in her lifetime, for decades her legacy was completely overshadowed by fellow nurse Florence Nightingale.

Since the centenary of her death in 1981 there's been an effort to make Seacole a household name. A statue of her was erected outside St Thomas' Hospital and in 2004 she was voted the greatest black Briton. But there has also been controversy.

Academics, medical professionals and concerned parties have fought the narrative that Seacole was a worthy nursing contemporary of Nightingale's. Seacole's methods were denigrated by some to nothing more than selling beverages to onlookers. Unsurprisingly, this has caused further backlash from those who believe her contribution to nursing is being minimised due to racism.

Women throughout history have had to deal with having their achievements minimised and judged against accepted white supremacist patriarchal capitalist ideals. Well, I'm calling it, Mrs Seacole is a hero, and there's room for both Seacole and Nightingale to be celebrated. And there's another reason to celebrate Seacole. She dealt with racist bullshit while also battling the sexism Nightingale did, as you'll see from her account of a speech she gave to a group of white men, who, when toasting her for ridding them of cholera, noted how they would bleach her if they could to make her more acceptable.

Gentlemen, – I return you my best thanks for your kindness in drinking my health. As for what I have done in Cruces, Providence evidently made me to be useful, and I can't help it. But I must say that I don't altogether appreciate your friend's kind wishes with respect to my complexion.

If it had been as dark as any nigger's, I should have been just as happy and as useful, and as much respected by those whose respect I value; and as to his offer of bleaching me, I should, even it were practicable, decline it without any thanks.

As to the society which the process might gain me admission into, all I can say is, that, judging from the specimens I have met with here and elsewhere, I don't think that I shall lose much by being excluded from it.

So, gentlemen, I drink to you and the general reformation of American manners.

MARY MCLEOD BETHUNE
(1875-1955)
WHAT AMERICAN DEMOCRACY MEANS TO ME

Arguably the most influential African-American woman in the 20th century, Bethune was born to two former slaves and went on to be a friend to President Roosevelt and First Lady Eleanor. An educator who founded a school and the UNCF (fund for African-American college students), she was the only woman member of the 'Black Cabinet'.

It's 1939, Jim Crow laws continue to be upheld across the US. That meant segregation in all areas of public life. It meant the state sanctioned abuse of African-Americans and fuelled the KKK in their reign of terror. It was also the era of radio. Voices could reach further than ever, including Bethune's.

On 23rd November 1939, she was invited to take part in one of the first chat shows, *America's Town Meeting of the Air*, where speakers were invited to talk for ten minutes. She took the opportunity to show up the US so-called democracy, and described what the dream of democracy could look like, almost three decades before Martin Luther King delivered his famous *I Have A Dream* speech.

Democracy is for me, and for 12 million black Americans, a goal towards which our nation is marching. It is a dream and an ideal in whose ultimate realisation we have a deep and abiding faith. For me, it is based on Christianity, in which we confidently entrust our destiny as a people. Under God's guidance in this great democracy, we are rising out of the darkness of slavery into the light of freedom. Here my race has been afforded [the] opportunity to advance from a people 80% illiterate to a people 80% literate; from abject poverty to the ownership and operation of a million farms and 750,000 homes; from total disenfranchisement to participation in government; from the status of chattels to recognised contributors to the American culture.

As we have been extended a measure of democracy, we have brought to the nation rich gifts. We have helped to build America with our labour, strengthened it with our faith and enriched it with our song. We have given you Paul Laurence Dunbar, Booker T Washington, Marian Anderson and George Washington Carver. But even these are only the first fruits of a rich harvest, which will be reaped when new and wider fields are opened to us.

The democratic doors of equal opportunity have not been opened wide to Negroes. In the Deep South, Negro youth is offered only one-fifteenth of the educational opportunity of the average American child. The great masses of Negro workers are depressed and unprotected in the lowest levels of agriculture and domestic service, while the black workers in industry are barred from certain unions and generally assigned to the more laborious and poorly paid work. Their housing and living conditions are sordid and unhealthy. They live too often in terror of the lynch mob; are deprived too often of the Constitutional right of suffrage; and are humiliated too often by the denial of civil liberties. We do not believe that justice and common decency will allow these conditions to continue.

Our faith in visions of fundamental change as mutual respect and understanding between our races come in the path of spiritual awakening.

Certainly there have been times when we may have delayed this mutual understanding by being slow to assume a fuller share of our national responsibility because of the denial of full equality. And yet, we have always been loyal when the ideals of American democracy have been attacked.

We have given our blood in its defence – from Crispus Attucks on Boston Commons to the battlefields of France. We have fought for the democratic principles of equality under the law, equality of opportunity, equality at the ballot box, for the guarantees of life, liberty and the pursuit of happiness. We have fought to preserve one nation, conceived in liberty and dedicated to the proposition that all men are created equal. Yes, we have fought for America with all her imperfections, not so much for what she is, but for what we know she can be.

Perhaps the greatest battle is before us, the fight for a new America: fearless, free, united, morally re-armed, in which 12 million Negroes, shoulder to shoulder with their fellow Americans, will strive that this nation under God will have a new birth of freedom, and that government of the people, for the people and by the people shall not perish from the earth. This dream, this idea, this aspiration, this is what American democracy means to me.

DIANE ABBOTT MP

(1953–)

ONLINE ABUSE

Almost a century later and the UK's first black woman MP, and longest serving black MP, Diane Abbott, has been in Parliament for three decades, playing an important role in our democracy. She was born to working-class Jamaican parents, went to a grammar school and then to Cambridge University to study History. In contrast to Bethune's era, this appears to be the dream realised. A black working-class woman able to access the best in education and represent her country in a parliamentary democracy, but although the laws have changed, culture hasn't.

In 2017 Amnesty International found that of all the abusive tweets sent to female MPs in the run-up to the general election, almost half were sent to Abbott. The speech below is from a Westminster Hall debate in July 2017, where Abbott stood up and exposed the abuse and intimidation she receives on a daily basis, just for daring to be a black woman in public life, abuse she believes has got worse since the advent of anonymous social media platforms like Twitter.

We are not talking here about robust debate, however robust it is. We are talking about mindless abuse. And in my case, the mindless abuse has been characteristically racist and sexist. And just to outline – I've had death threats, I've had people tweeting that I should be hung, if, quote, 'they could find a tree big enough to take the fat bitch's weight'.

There was an EDL [English Defence League] affiliated twitter account – #burnDianeAbbott. I've had rape threats, described as 'a pathetic useless fat black piece of shit', 'ugly fat black bitch' and 'nigger' – nigger over and over again. And my members of staff said that when people ask them what is the most surprising thing about coming to work for me, the most surprising thing for them is how often they have to read the word 'nigger'.

And this comes in through emails, through Twitter, through Facebook.

But where I disagree with the honourable gentleman, he seems to suggest that this is all a relatively recent thing around our time at this election. Um, that's not my experience, that really is not my experience.

It is certainly true that online abuse, the online abuse that I experience and others experience, has got worse in recent years and it does get worse at election time. But I don't put it down to a particular election.

I think the rise in the use of online [media] has turbo-charged abuse, because, you know, 30 years ago, when I became an MP, if you wanted to attack an MP, you had to write a letter, usually in green ink, you had to put it in an envelope, you'd have to put a stamp on it, and you had to walk to a post box.

Now they press a button and you read vile abuse which 30 years ago people would have been frightened to even write down.

So I said that male politicians get abused too, but I hope the one thing we can agree on in this chamber is that it is much worse for women. And I think as well as the rise of online, anonymity is the thing. People would not come up to me and attack me for being a nigger in public, but they'll do it online. I'm telling you this isn't once a week, this isn't during election, this is every day.

JACINDA ARDERN PM

(1980–)

YOU WILL NEVER HEAR ME MENTION HIS NAME

Now, why is there a white voice in a chapter on race? Well, I don't think white supremacy is for people of colour to solve alone. White people need to take responsibility. In March 2019, after the attacks on two mosques in Christchurch by a white supremacist, I think New Zealand Prime Minister Ardern demanded that of us all.

It's become unfashionable to be liberal like Ardern. A bit cheesy. Bit too PC. The pictures of her wearing a headscarf after the mosque attacks were mocked in right-wing areas of Twitter and the media. She emulates the cheesiest of all the so-called centrist liberals Tony Blair, whom she was an advisor to while he was in government. But this is a woman who puts her heart where her mouth is. She even left her Mormon church because it didn't align with her belief in LGBT rights.

Wouldn't you prefer politicians to hug and to empathise with victims of white supremacy? It's their duty to call out racism and back up that call-out with action, like gun control.

Mr Speaker, *Al salam Alaikum*. Peace be upon you. And peace be upon all of us.

Mr Speaker, March 15th will now be forever a day etched in our collective memories. On a quiet Friday afternoon, a man stormed into a place of peaceful worship and took away the lives of 50 people. That quiet Friday afternoon has become our darkest of days. But for the families, it was more than that. It was the day that the simple act of prayer – of practising their Muslim faith and religion – led to the loss of their loved ones' lives.

Those loved ones were brothers, daughters, fathers and children. They were New Zealanders. They are us. And because they are us, we, as a nation, we mourn them.

One of the roles I never anticipated having, and hoped never to have, is to voice the grief of a nation. At this time, it has been second only to securing the care of those affected and the safety of everyone. And in this role, I wanted to speak directly to the families.

We cannot know your grief, but we can walk with you at every stage. We can. And we will surround you with *aroha, manaakitanga* and all that makes us, us. Our hearts are heavy but our spirit is strong.

Mr Speaker, six minutes after a 111 call was placed alerting the police to the shootings at Al-Noor mosque, police were on the scene. The arrest itself was nothing short of an act of bravery. Two country police officers rammed the vehicle from which the offender was still shooting. They pulled open his car door – when there were explosives inside – and pulled him out. I know we all wish to acknowledge that their acts put the safety of New Zealanders above their own and we thank them.

But they were not the only ones who showed extraordinary courage. Naeem Rashid, originally from Pakistan, died after rushing at the terrorist and trying to wrestle the gun from him. He lost his life trying to save those who were worshipping alongside him.

Abdul Aziz, originally from Afghanistan, confronted and faced down the armed terrorist after grabbing the nearest thing to hand – a simple eftpos [electronic funds transfer] machine. He risked his life and no doubt saved many with his selfless bravery.

For many of us, the first sign of the scale of this terrorist attack was the images of ambulance staff transporting victims to Christchurch hospital. To the first responders, the ambulance staff and the health professionals who have assisted, and who continue to assist those who have been injured, please accept the heartfelt thanks of us all. I saw first-hand your care and your professionalism in the face of extraordinary challenges. We are proud of your work, and incredibly grateful for it.

Mr Speaker, if you'll allow, I'd like to talk about some of the immediate measures currently in place especially to ensure the safety of our Muslim community, and more broadly the safety of everyone.

As a nation, we do remain on high alert. While there isn't a specific threat at present, we are maintaining vigilance. Unfortunately, we have seen in countries that know the horrors of terrorism more than us, there is a pattern of increased tension and actions over the weeks that follow that means we do need to ensure that vigilance is maintained.

There is an additional and ongoing security presence in Christchurch, and as the police have indicated, there will continue to be a police presence at mosques around the country while their doors are open. When they are closed, police will be in the vicinity.

There is a huge focus on ensuring the needs of families are met. That has to be our priority. A community welfare centre has been set up near the hospital in Christchurch to make sure people know how to access support. Visas for family members overseas are being prioritised so that they can attend funerals. Funeral costs are covered, and we have moved quickly to ensure that this includes repatriation costs for any family members who would like to move their loved ones away from New Zealand. We are working to provide mental health and social support.

I know though, Mr Speaker, that there have rightly been questions around how this could have happened here. In a place that prides itself on being open, peaceful, diverse. And there is anger that it has happened here. There are many questions that need to be answered, and the assurance that I give you is that they will be.

Yesterday, Cabinet agreed that an inquiry – one that looks into the events that led up to the attack on March 15th – will occur. We will examine what we did know, could have known, or should have known. We cannot allow this to happen again. Part of ensuring the safety of New Zealanders must include a frank examination of our gun laws.

As I have already said, Mr Speaker, our gun laws will change. Cabinet met yesterday and made in-principle decisions, 72 hours after the attack. Before we meet again next Monday, these decisions will be announced.

A 28-year-old man – an Australian citizen – has been charged with one count of murder. Other charges will follow. He will face the full force of the law in New Zealand. The families of the fallen will have justice. He sought many things from his act of terror, but one was notoriety. And that is why you will never hear me mention his name.

He is a terrorist. He is a criminal. He is an extremist. But he will, when I speak, be nameless. And to others, I implore you: speak the names of those who were lost, rather than the name of the man who took them. He may have sought notoriety, but we in New Zealand will give him nothing. Not even his name.

Mr Speaker, we will also look at the role social media played and what steps we can take, including on the international stage, and in unison with our partners. There is no question that ideas and language of division and hate have existed for decades, but their form of distribution, the tools of organisation, they are new. We cannot simply sit back and accept that these platforms just exist and that what is said on them is not the responsibility of the place where they are published. They are the publisher. Not just the postman. There cannot be a case of all profit, no responsibility.

I don't have all of the answers now, but we must collectively find them. And we must act.

As I conclude, I acknowledge there are many stories that will have struck all of us since March 15th. One I wish to mention is that of Hati Mohemmed Daoud Nabi. He was the 71-year-old man who opened the door at the Al-Noor mosque and uttered the words, 'Hello brother, welcome.' His final words. Of course, he had no idea of the hate that sat behind the door, but his welcome tells us so much – that he was a member of a faith that welcomed all its members, that showed openness and care.

I have said many times, Mr Speaker, we are a nation of 200 ethnicities, 160 languages. We open our doors to others and say welcome. And the only thing that must change after the events of Friday is that this same door must close on all of those who espouse hate and fear.

We wish for every member of our communities to also feel safe. Safety means being free from the fear of violence. But it also means being free from the fear of those sentiments of racism and hate that create a place where violence can flourish. And every single one of us has the power to change that.

Mr Speaker, on Friday it will be a week since the attack. Members of the Muslim community will gather for worship on that day. Let us acknowledge their grief as they do. Let's support them as they gather again for worship. We are one, they are us.

Tatau tatau, Al salam Alaikum, Weh Rahmat Allah, Weh Barakaatuh.

CHAPTER 6
WAR & TAXES

'Aren't you a little short for
a Stormtrooper?'
Princess Leia

I hated history at school. It was all war and taxes, and the word
feudal still makes me feel sick. Of course, when you're proper
adulting, war and taxes become a little more relatable. You care
about how the healthcare system is funded. You go on marches
to stop wars. You might even fight in them.

Well, some of the biggest and most well-known women in
history banged on about war and taxes. It's easy to forget that
even throughout a history where most women were prevented
from holding positions of power, through birth or marriage
many often ended up leading armies and governments.

Here are history's greatest rallying cries from women.
Including Queens and religious fundamentalists. If you ever

need to rally a team or need a pep talk before going into your own battles, you can find army-rousing turns of phrase here.

We end by questioning the glamour and romance for battle these Queens share, with a critical poem about the horror of modern warfare by Kate Tempest.

QUEEN ELIZABETH I

(1533–1603)

SPEECH TO THE TROOPS AT TILBURY

Being Queen Elizabeth I must have been complicated. There's a lot of death. First, your dad beheads your mum, then your dad dies. You're imprisoned by your older sister Mary I. You become Queen after her death. Parliament want you to marry, you refuse. Your cousin Mary, Queen of Scots is a threat to you, so in the family tradition you behead her. All the while you're fighting the threat of invasion from the Spanish. You die known as the Virgin Queen.

This speech was recorded in a letter from Leonel Sharp to the Duke of Buckingham. There are other versions, and disagreements over whether they are accurate or not. Regardless of the accuracy, it contains one of the most famous soundbites from women's history: 'I know I have the body but of a weak and feeble woman, but I have the heart and stomach of a King.'

Elizabeth joined the camp of soldiers based in Tilbury on the Thames estuary in Essex, readying themselves to take on the Spanish Armada. She arrived in a white gown, with helmet, to rally her troops. To inspire them. To win.

My loving people, We have been persuaded by some that are careful of our safety, to take heed how we commit ourselves to armed multitudes, for fear of treachery; but I assure you I do not desire to live to distrust my faithful and loving people. Let tyrants fear.

I have always so behaved myself that, under God, I have placed my chiefest strength and safeguard in the loyal hearts and good-will of my subjects; and therefore I am come amongst you, as you see, at this time, not for my recreation and disport, but being resolved, in the midst and heat of the battle, to live and die amongst you all; to lay down for my God, and for my kingdom, and my people, my honour and my blood, even in the dust.

I know I have the body but of a weak and feeble woman; but I have the heart and stomach of a king, and of a king of England too,

and think foul scorn that Parma or Spain, or any prince of Europe, should dare to invade the borders of my realm: to which rather than any dishonour shall grow by me, I myself will take up arms, I myself will be your general, judge, and rewarder of every one of your virtues in the field.

I know already, for your forwardness you have deserved rewards and crowns; and We do assure you in the word of a prince, they shall be duly paid you. In the mean time, my lieutenant general shall be in my stead, than whom never prince commanded a more noble or worthy subject; not doubting but by your obedience to my general, by your concord in the camp, and your valour in the field, we shall shortly have a famous victory over those enemies of my God, of my kingdom, and of my people.

BOUDICCA
(30AD–61AD)

From a winning Queen to a losing leader, Boudicca may have come to represent the warrior heart of Britain, fighting the Roman colonists, with a statue of her, aloft on a horse-drawn chariot, outside the Houses of Parliament. But the sad fact is we don't know much about Boudicca, what we do know isn't that flattering and all we know for sure is that she lost.

There are three accounts, two by Tacitus and one by Dio, both Roman historians, the Romans being Boudicca's sworn enemy. So it's not surprising if what we learn of Boudicca is a bit one-sided. They paint her as a wild, 'bestial', ruthless savage, overseeing the pillage of her enemies' towns, cutting off the breasts of Roman women and sewing them over their mouths.

These were savage times though, and Boudicca was rightly angry. Her English kingdom, which had been an ally of Rome's, was taken away from her when her husband died. Her daughters were raped. So, she led a rebellion of Britons that killed tens of thousands, and the Romans considered leaving the province, but in the end Boudicca lost against Suetonius, and either killed herself or died from illness, depending on which Roman historian you read.

Here we hear what, according to Tacitus, Boudicca said to Suetonius' troops, as she rode around with her daughters sitting on the front of her carriage, 'haranguing' them.

Britons had been wont to do battle under the leadership of women; but she was not now fighting for throne and power, as one sprung from royal ancestors, but as one of the multitude, to avenge the loss of liberty, the tripes inflicted upon her flesh, and the outrages perpetrated on her daughters.

Roman lust had grown so rampant that it left nothing undefiled; not even the persons of their old men or their young maidens.

But the Gods were there, to help on a just vengeance. The legion which had dared battle had been destroyed; the rest were skulking in their camp, or looking for a chance to flee: never would they endure the din and clamour, far less the onset and the blows, of so many thousands.

If they looked at the number of their armed men, and weighed well the causes of the war, they must conquer on that field or die. Such was a woman's resolve: men might live on and be slaves.

YAA ASANTEWAA

(1840–1921)

NOW I SEE

Like Boudicca, Asantewaa found herself in power and in battle because of the absence of strong male leadership and facing an aggressive colonial force. This time the British, in what became known as the War of the Golden Stool.

The British wanted to turn Asante Region into a colony. They exiled members of the leadership, including the King. Finally the British Governor demanded the Asante turn over the Golden Stool – the throne of Asante. The remaining members of the Asante government met to discuss what to do.

As Queen Mother, Asantewaa was present, and gave this now famous speech, shaming the men into action. With that she took leadership of thousands of troops, and pushed back against the British.

Now I see that some of you fear to go forward to fight for our King.

If it were in the brave days of Osei Tutu, Okomfo Anokye, and Opoku Ware, chiefs would not sit down to see their King to be taken away without firing a shot.

No European could have dared speak to chiefs of Asante in the way

the governor spoke to you this
morning.

Is it true that the bravery of Asante is no more? I
cannot believe it. It cannot be!

I must say this: if you, the men of Asante, will not go
forward, then we will. We, the women, will. I shall call upon
my fellow women. We will fight! We will fight till the last of
us falls in the battlefields.

HORTENSIA
(1st CENTURY BC)
WHY SHOULD WE PAY TAXES?

Do you enjoy paying your taxes? Happy about what the money is used for? Well, Hortensia had some very strong feelings.

The Roman Empire was by this point in turmoil. The Second Triumvirate (basically a leadership group of Marcus Antonius, Octavianus and Marcus Aemilius Lepidus) were at war with the assassins of Julius Caesar. To fund this war they resorted to proscription – state-sponsored murder – of wealthy citizens, taking all their money. When that still wasn't enough cash, they took to taxing the wealthiest women.

Hortensia did not want to pay, so she led a group of equally unhappy women to the Roman Forum and gave this speech.

Why should we pay taxes when we have no part in the honours, the commands, the state-craft, for which you contend against each other with such harmful results?

'Because this is a time of war,' do you say?

When have there not been wars, and when have taxes ever been imposed on women, who are exempted by their sex among all mankind?

Our mothers did once rise superior to their sex and made contributions when you were in danger of losing the whole empire and the city itself through the conflict with the Carthaginians. But then they contributed voluntarily, not from their landed property, their fields, their dowries, or their houses, without which life is not possible to free women, but only from their own jewellery, and even these not according to the fixed valuation, not under fear of informers or accusers, not by force and violence, but what they themselves were willing to give.

What alarm is there now for the empire or the country? Let war with the Gauls or the Parthians come, and we shall not be inferior to our mothers in zeal for the common safety; but for civil wars may we never contribute, nor ever assist you against each other!

JOAN OF ARC
(1412–1431)
TRIAL

Joan of Arc is, like Boudicca, a folk hero. Also like Boudicca, she is a complicated hero, because Joan of Arc was essentially a religious extremist, in a world of religious extremists.

She was born into a peasant family in Domrémy in France, and rose to be canonised as a Roman Catholic saint, although she only lived for 19 years. Joan said she saw visions of archangels and saints, who instructed her to help the French King Charles VII in the Hundred Years' War with the English. The King sent Joan to the battle, where she wore men's clothes.

But she was caught and put on trial by the English. Here is an excerpt from her trial. In its entirety it's a painful read. Here's a really young, sometimes confused, sometimes strong woman, being asked the same questions again and again and again by some very hostile bishops. She can't win, and she didn't. She was found guilty and burnt at the stake.

Asked whether that night the voice had not advised her what she should reply, she said that if the voice revealed it she did not well understand. Asked whether a light was visible on the last two days that she heard voices, she answered that the light comes in the name of the voice. Asked whether she saw anything with this voice, she answered: 'I will not tell you everything and I have no permission for that', for her oath did not touch on that. She said the voice is beautiful, good and worthy, and she is not bound to answer what she is asked. Asked whether the voice had sight or eyes (this was asked because she desired to have in writing the points on which she did not reply), she answered: 'You will not learn that yet', in French, *'Vous ne l'avez pas encore'*.

She said that little children have a proverb, 'Men are sometimes hanged for telling the truth.'

...

On the Tuesday, February 27th, when we required the said Jeanne to take an oath and swear to speak the truth on questions concerning the trial, she answered that she would willingly swear in respect of the questions concerning her case, but not of all she knew. Then we required her to answer truthfully everything she should be asked. She replied as before, saying, 'You ought to be satisfied. I have sworn enough.' She said she would willingly speak the truth concerning subjects for which she had leave from Our Lord, but without the permission of her voice she will not tell the revelations concerning her King. The same day, asked whether St Catherine and St Margaret were dressed in the same cloth, she said: 'I will not tell you any more now', for she had not permission to reveal it; and 'if you don't believe me, go to Poitiers.'

She said certain revelations came to her King and not to those who questioned her. Asked if the saints who appeared to her were of the same age, she said she had not leave to tell. Asked whether they spoke at the same time, or one after another, she said she may not tell, but every day she had counsel of both. Asked which first appeared to her, she answered: 'I did not recognise them immediately'; once she knew well enough, but has now forgotten. If she is permitted she will willingly tell: it is written down at Poitiers. Asked in what form St Michael appeared to her she said: 'There is as yet no reply to that, for I have not leave to answer.' Asked what St Michael said to her the first time, she answered: 'You will get no further reply to-day.' She says the voices told her to answer boldly, and added that she has not yet leave to reveal what St Michael told her; and wishes her examiner had a copy of the book at Poitiers, if it were God's will. Asked if St Michael and the other saints told her she must not reveal them without their leave, she said: 'I still may not answer', and, 'What I have permission to, I will gladly answer', and if the voices forbade her, she did not understand them. Asked what sign she gives that this revelation comes from God, and that it is St Catherine and St Margaret who speak to her, she answered: 'I have told you often enough that it is St Catherine and St Margaret', and, 'Believe me if you will'. Asked what revelations the King had, she answered: 'You will not learn from me this year.'

On Thursday, March 1st, asked what the saints promised her, she answered: 'That is not in your case at all.' Asked if they promised her anything beyond that they would lead her to Paradise, she answered that there were other promises but she will not tell them, they do not concern the trial. Within three months she will tell the other promises. Asked if the saints said that within three months she should be delivered out of prison, she answered: 'That is not in your case.' Nevertheless, she does not know when she will be delivered. She says that they who want to get her out of this world may well go before her. Asked whether her counsel had not told her she would be delivered from gaol, she answered: 'Speak to me of it in three months' time; I will answer you.' She added that we should ask the assessors on their oath whether it concerned the trial, and after they had deliberated and unanimously decided that it did, she said: 'One day I must be delivered, and I want permission to tell you', and so asked for delay. Asked whether the saints forbade her to speak the truth, she answered: 'Do you want me to tell you what is the concern of the King of France?' She said many things do not concern her case. The same day, asked what sign she gave the King that she came from God, she said: 'I have always told you, you will not drag this from my lips. Go and ask him.' Asked if she had sworn not to reveal what she was asked concerning the trial, she answered: 'I have already told you that I will not tell you what concerns our King.' Asked if she did not know the sign, she answered: 'You will not learn it from me.' She was told that it concerned the trial, and answered: 'What I have promised to keep secret I shall not tell you', and added: 'I have already declared that I could not tell you without perjury.' Asked to whom she made the promise, she answered that she promised St Catherine and St Margaret, and this was shown to her King. She said she promised without their asking, of her own accord, and said that too many people would have asked her about the sign, had she not made this promise to her saints. Asked whether anyone else was present when she showed the sign to the King, she said: 'I think there was no one but him, although many people were quite near.' Asked if she saw the crown on her King's head, when she showed him the sign, she answered: 'I cannot tell you without perjury.'

On Saturday, March 3rd, asked whether she believes God created St Michael and St Gabriel from the beginning in the form and fashion in which she saw them, she answered: 'You will learn no more at present from me than I have told you.' Asked whether she had seen or known by revelation that she would escape, she answered: "That does not concern your case. Do you want me to speak against myself?' Asked if the voices told her anything of it, she said: 'That is not in your case. I leave it to Our Lord, and if everything concerned you, I would tell you everything.'

KATE TEMPEST

(1985–)

BALLAD OF A HERO

From a young French woman who died for going to war, to a modern-day Londoner who is critical of its destructive force on soldiers' lives. Tempest is a multi-award winning poet, rapper and playwright, born in London. A masterful communicator, filled with passion, her work is often highly political. And *Ballad of a Hero* is no exception. Here is a contemporary woman's voice on the damaging effects of war.

> Your Daddy is a soldier son,
> Your Daddy's gone to War,
> His steady hands they hold his gun,
> His aim is keen and sure.
>
> Your Daddy's in the desert now,
> The darkness and the dust,
> He's fighting for his country, yes,
> He's doing it for us.
>
> Your Daddy's coming home soon though,
> Not long now till he's back,
> We'll dress you in your smartest shirt
> And meet him down the track.

He'll put you on his shoulders and
You'll sing and clap and laugh,
I'll wrap my arms around his waist,
And hold him close at last.

Your Dad ain't left the house again,
Your Dad ain't brushed his teeth,
Your Dad keeps getting angry son,
At nights he doesn't sleep.

He's having his bad dreams again,
He seems worn out and weak,
I've tried to be there for him, but
We barely even speak.

He can't think what to say to me,
He don't know how to tell it,
Won medals for his bravery,
But just wants to forget it.

He's drinking more than ever son,
Before, he never cried.
But now, I wake at night and feel
Him shaking by my side.

He spoke to me at last my son!
He turned to me in tears,
I held him close and kissed his face
And asked him what he feared.

He said it's getting darker,
It hasn't disappeared,
And I can see it sharper
Now the sand and smoke have cleared.

There was this kid he'd got to know.
Young boy. Just turned 18,
Bright and kind, his name was Joe,
He kept his rifle clean.

Joe's girlfriend was expecting,
Joe loved to joke and laugh,
Joe marched in front of your old man,
As they patrolled a path.

Everything was quiet until
They heard the dreaded blast.
The man that marched in front of Joe
Was completely blown apart.

Some shrapnel hit Joe in the face,
Gouged both eyes at once,
The last thing those eyes ever saw
Was the man in front:

Limbs and flesh and bone and blood,
Torn up and thrown around,
And after that – just blackness.
The taste, the stink, the sound.

I tell you this my son, because
I know what you'll be like,
As soon as you've grown old enough
You'll want to go and fight

In whatever battle needs you,
You'll pledge your blood and bone,
Not in the name of good or evil –
But in the name of home.

Your Dad believes in fighting.
He fights for you and I,
But the men that send the armies in
Will never hear him cry.

I don't support the war, my son,

I don't believe it's right,

But I do support the soldiers who

Go off to war to fight.

Troops just like your daddy son,

Soldiers through and through,

Who wear their uniform with pride,

And do what they're told to do.

When you're grown, my sweet, my love,

Please don't go fighting wars,

But fight the men that start them

Or fight a cause that's yours.

It seems so full of honour, yes,

So valiant, so bold,

But the men that send the armies in

Send them in for gold,

Or they send them in for oil,

And they tell us it's for Britain

But the men come home like Daddy,

And spend their days just drinking.

CHAPTER 7
POLITICS

'Being nice should never be perceived as being weak.'
Benazir Bhutto, Prime Minister, Pakistan

My best friend voted for Brexit. I voted Remain. We both have strong opinions and aren't afraid to voice them, and yet we can still go on holiday together. I don't know what all these idiots are doing on the telly, but they aren't conducting politics as well as us. Maybe they need to do more karaoke?

Sadly, politics is far removed from karaoke. The difference is not hitting the high note in Sia's *Chandelier* after a couple of piña coladas; the difference is power. Politics over an 'all you can eat' buffet in Portugal isn't about having power over one another – although I will fight you for the last piece of calamari. Politics on the telly is all about power. It is the system of gaining and staying in power and historically, women have been excluded from it. We didn't create the political system.

But we are trying to navigate it, and lead in it, in ever greater numbers. There are record numbers of women serving in governments across the world. Eleven women are serving as Head of State, 12 as Head of Government. Three countries have more women than men in Parliament, with Rwanda leading in representation with 61% of seats in its lower house going to women, followed by Cuba and Bolivia.

Let's not get carried away though. Women are still woefully under-represented. There are many barriers, from imposter syndrome to having kids, from bias to preferring to avoid the abuse slung at politicians. Any woman going into politics is brave. Including ALL the women in this chapter, regardless of whether I would ever have voted for them.

Our first two speeches are from women at the beginning of their political careers. Idealistic, hopeful and unedited by experience. Hillary Rodham's graduation speech, before she became a Clinton and long before Trump called her a 'Nasty Woman'. Mhairi Black's maiden speech in the British Parliament as the youngest ever parliamentarian.

Followed by three women at the height of their power, fully entrenched in familiar arguments and counter arguments. The UK's first communist mayor, Annie Powell, on her solutions to poverty. Our first female Prime Minister, Margaret Thatcher, on Europe, Russia, Afghanistan and the threat from a Marxist Labour at a time when there was a celebrity in the White House. And Margaret Smith, the first woman to be placed in nomination for the presidency at a major party's convention in the US, demanding politicians stop psychologically dividing the country.

All three offer us some perspective on our current political landscape, and beg the question – are we repeating ourselves?

HILLARY RODHAM CLINTON

(1947–)

1969 STUDENT COMMENCEMENT SPEECH

Hillary Rodham Clinton means a lot of things to a lot of people. Winner of the popular vote and almost the US's first woman president. The First Wife who poured doubt on the women who accused her husband of being a philanderer. Nasty woman. The lawyer. The grandma. Warmonger. Snazzy pantsuit wearer.

She was obviously going to be in this book. She's played a huge role in global politics for the past 30 years. But I wanted to know what she was like before politics. Before the donors and the smiles for the press, before she'd lost out to Obama and then to Trump.

A life played out in the political limelight will change you. So much training, mistakes made in the public glare and a tool box of clever rhetoric. Below is a speech she gave upon graduating from Wellesley College in 1969. She reveals the reasons why she loves politics, the subject she majored in, and the values that guide her: integrity, trust and respect.

Ruth M Adams, ninth president of Wellesley College, introduced Hillary D Rodham.

'In addition to inviting Senator Brooke to speak to them this morning, the Class of '69 has expressed a desire [for a student] to speak to them and for them at this morning's commencement. There was no debate so far as I could ascertain as to who their spokesman was to be: Miss Hillary Rodham. Member of this graduating class, she is a major in political science and a candidate for the degree with honours. In four years she has combined academic ability with active service to the College, her junior year having served as a Vil Junior, and then as a member of Senate and during the past year as president of College Government and presiding officer of College Senate. She is also cheerful, good humoured, good company, and a good friend to all of us and it is a great pleasure to present to this audience Miss Hillary Rodham.'

We're not in the positions yet of leadership and power, but we do have that indispensable element of criticising and constructive protest and I find myself reacting just briefly to some of the things that Senator Brooke said. This has to be quick because I do have a little speech to give.

Part of the problem with just empathy with professed goals is that empathy doesn't do us anything. We've had lots of empathy; we've had lots of sympathy, but we feel that for too long our leaders have viewed politics as the art of the possible. And the challenge now is to practise politics as the art of making what appears to be impossible possible. What does it mean to hear that 13.3% of the people in this country are below the poverty line? That's a percentage. We're not interested in social reconstruction; it's human reconstruction. How can we talk about percentages and trends? The complexities are not lost in our analyses, but perhaps they're just put into what we consider a more human and eventually a more progressive perspective.

The question about possible and impossible was one that we brought with us to Wellesley four years ago. We arrived not yet knowing what was not possible. Consequently, we expected a lot. Our attitudes are easily understood having grown up, having come to consciousness in the first five years of this decade – years dominated by men with dreams, men in the civil rights movement, the Peace Corps, the space programme – so we arrived at Wellesley and we found, as all of us have found, that there was a gap between expectation and realities. But it wasn't a discouraging gap and it didn't turn us into cynical, bitter old women at the age of 18. It just inspired us to do something about that gap. What we did is often difficult for some people to understand. They ask us quite often: 'Why, if you're dissatisfied, do you stay in a place?' Well, if you didn't care a lot about it you wouldn't stay. It's almost as though my mother used to say, 'You know I'll always love you but there are times when I certainly won't like you.' Our love for this place, this particular place, Wellesley College, coupled with our freedom from the burden of an inauthentic reality allowed us to question basic assumptions underlying our education.

We are, all of us, exploring a world that none of us even understands and attempting to create within that uncertainty. But there are some things we feel, feelings that our prevailing, acquisitive and competitive corporate life, including tragically the universities, is not the way of life for us. We're searching for more immediate, ecstatic, and penetrating modes of living. And so our questions, our questions about our institutions, about our colleges, about our churches, about our government, continue. The questions about those institutions are familiar to all of us. We have seen them heralded across the newspapers. Senator Brooke has suggested some of them this morning. But along with using these words – integrity, trust, and respect – in regard to institutions and leaders, we're perhaps harshest with them in regard to ourselves.

We ... know that to be educated, the goal of it must be human liberation. A liberation enabling each of us to fulfil our capacity so as to be free to create within and around ourselves. To be educated to freedom must be evidenced in action, and here again is where we ask ourselves, as we have asked our parents and our teachers, questions about integrity, trust and respect. Those three words mean different things to all of us. Some of the things they can mean, for instance: Integrity, the courage to be whole, to try to mould an entire person in this particular context, living in relation to one another in the full poetry of existence.

If the only tool we have ultimately to use is our lives, so we use it in the way we can by choosing a way to live that will demonstrate the way we feel and the way we know.

Trust. This is one word that when I asked the class at our rehearsal what it was they wanted me to say for them, everyone came up to me and said 'Talk about trust, talk about the lack of trust both for us and the way we feel about others. Talk about the trust bust.' What can you say about it? What can you say about a feeling that permeates a generation and that perhaps is not even understood by those who are distrusted? All we can do is keep trying again and again and again. There's that wonderful line in *East Coker* by [TS] Eliot about there's only the trying, again and again and again; to win again what we've lost before.

And then Respect. There's that mutuality of respect between people where you don't see people as percentage points. Where you don't manipulate people. Where you're not interested in social engineering for people. The struggle for an integrated life existing in an atmosphere of communal trust and respect is one with desperately important political and social consequences. And the word conse-quences of course catapults us into the future. One of the most tragic things that happened yesterday, a beautiful day, was that I was talking to a woman who said that she wouldn't want to be me for anything in the world. She wouldn't want to live today and look ahead to what it is she sees because she's afraid. Fear is always with us but we just don't have time for it. Not now.

There are two people that I would like to thank before concluding. That's Eldie Acheson, who is the spearhead for this, and also Nancy Scheibner who wrote this poem which is the last thing that I would like to read:

My entrance into the world of so-called 'social problems'
Must be with quiet laughter, or not at all.
The hollow men of anger and bitterness
The bountiful ladies of righteous degradation
All must be left to a bygone age.
And the purpose of history is to provide a receptacle
For all those myths and oddments
Which oddly we have acquired
And from which we would become unburdened
To create a newer world
To translate the future into the past.
We have no need of false revolutions

In a world where categories tend to tyrannise our
   minds
And hang our wills up on narrow pegs.
It is well at every given moment to seek the limits in
   our lives.
And once those limits are understood
To understand that limitations no longer exist.
Earth could be fair. And you and I must be free
Not to save the world in a glorious crusade
Not to kill ourselves with a nameless gnawing pain
But to practise with all the skill of our being
The art of making possible.

Thanks.

MHAIRI BLACK MP

(1994–)

MAIDEN SPEECH

From one of the first speeches from one of the world's greatest stateswomen, to the maiden speech from Westminster's youngest ever MP, aka The Baby of the House, Mhairi Black. When elected she was just 20 and still had her final exam to sit on her politics degree. As a Scottish National Party MP candidate she defeated a Labour MP when their vote collapsed in the 2015 election.

Black is a Socialist and fierce LGBTQI campaigner. Here is how she began her time in Parliament. She has since claimed it takes too long to get anything done in Westminster, saying 'A lot of the time, it is just a waste of time.'

Firstly in my maiden speech I want to pay tribute to my predecessor, Douglas Alexander. He served the constituency for many years. After all, I was only three when he was elected. But it is because of that fact that I want to thank him for all he did for the constituency and I especially want to take a moment to commend him for the dignified way that he handled himself on what must have been a very difficult election night. He did himself proud, he did his party proud, and I wish him the best for the future.

Now, when I discovered it is tradition to speak about the history of your constituency in a maiden speech, I decided to do some research despite the fact I've lived there all my life. And as one of the tail end doing the maiden speech of my colleagues in the SNP I've noticed that my colleagues quite often mention Rabbie Burns a lot and they all try to form this intrinsic connection between him and their own constituency and own him for themselves. I, however, feel no need to do this, for during my research I discovered a fact which trumps them all. William Wallace was born in my constituency.

Now, my constituency has a fascinating history far beyond the Hollywood film and historical name. From the mills of Paisley, to the industries of Johnstone, right to the weavers in Kilbarchan, it's got a wonderful population with a cracking sense of humour and much to offer both the tourists and to those who reside there. But the truth is that within my constituency it's not all fantastic. We've watched our town centres deteriorate. We've watched our communities decline. Our unemployment level is higher than that of the UK average. One in five children in my constituency go to bed hungry every night. Paisley Job Centre has the third highest number of sanctions in the whole of Scotland.

Before I was elected I volunteered for a charitable organisation and there was a gentleman who I grew very fond of. He was one of these guys who has been battered by life in every way imaginable. You name it, he's been through it. And he used to come in to get food from this charity, and it was the only food that he had access to and it was the only meal he would get. And I sat with him and he told me about his fear of going to the Job Centre. He said, 'I've heard the stories, Mhairi. They try and trick you out, they'll tell you you're a liar. I'm not a liar, Mhairi, I'm not.' And I told him 'It's OK, calm down. Go, be honest, it'll be fine.'

I then didn't see him for about two or three weeks. I did get very worried, and when he finally did come back in I said to him, 'How did you get on?'

And without saying a word he burst into tears. That grown man standing in front of a 20-year-old crying his eyes out, because what had happened to him was the money that he would normally use to pay for his travel to come to the charity to get his food, he decided that in order to afford to get to the Job Centre, he would save that money. Because of this, he didn't eat for five days, he didn't drink. When he was on the bus on the way to the Job Centre, he fainted due to exhaustion and dehydration. He was 15 minutes late for the Job Centre and he was sanctioned for 13 weeks.

Now, when the Chancellor spoke in his budget about fixing the roof while the sun is shining, I would have to ask on whom is the sun shining? When he spoke about benefits not supporting certain kinds of lifestyles, is that the kind of lifestyle that he was talking about?

If we go back even further when the Minister for Employment was asked to consider if there was a correlation between the number of sanctions and the rise in food bank use she stated, and I quote, 'Food banks play an important role in local welfare provision.' Renfrewshire has the third highest use of food banks and food bank use is going up and up.

> Food banks are not part of the welfare state, they are a symbol that the welfare state is failing.

Now, the Government quite rightly pays for me through taxpayers' money to be able to live in London whilst I serve my constituents. My housing is subsidised by the taxpayer. Now, the Chancellor in his budget said it is not fair that families earning over £40,000 in London should have their rents paid for by other working people. But it is OK so long as you're an MP? In this budget the Chancellor also abolished any housing benefit for anyone below the age of 21. So we are now in the ridiculous situation whereby because I am an MP not only am I the youngest, but I am also the only 20-year-old in the whole of the UK that the Chancellor is prepared to help with housing. We now have one of the most uncaring, uncompromising and out of touch governments that the UK has seen since Thatcher.

It is here now that I must turn to those who I share a bench with. Now I have [been] in this chamber for ten weeks, and I have very deliberately stayed quiet and have listened intently to everything that has been said. I have heard multiple speeches from Labour benches standing to talk about the worrying rise of nationalism in Scotland, when in actual fact all these speeches have served to do is to demonstrate how deep the lack of understanding about Scotland is within the Labour party.

I, like many SNP members, come from a traditional socialist Labour family and I have never been quiet in my assertion that I feel that it is the Labour party that left me, not the other way about. The SNP did not triumph on a wave of nationalism; in fact nationalism has nothing to do with what's happened in Scotland. We triumphed on a wave of hope, hope that there was something different, something better than the Thatcherite neo-liberal policies that are produced from this chamber. Hope that representatives genuinely could give a voice to those who don't have one.

I don't mention this in order to pour salt into wounds which I am sure are very open and very sore for many members on these benches, both politically and personally. Colleagues, possibly friends, have lost their seats. I mention it in order to hold a mirror to the face of a party that seems to have forgotten the very people they're supposed to represent, the very things they're supposed to fight for.

After hearing the Labour leader's intentions to support the changes of tax credits that the Chancellor has put forward, I must make this plea to the words of one of your own and a personal hero of mine. Tony Benn once said that in politics there are weathercocks and signposts. Weathercocks will spin in whatever direction the wind of public opinion may blow them, no matter what principle they may have to compromise. And then there are signposts; signposts which stand true and tall and principled. And they point in the direction and they say this is the way to a better society and it is my job to convince you why. Tony Benn was right when he said the only people worth remembering in politics were signposts.

Now, yes, we will have political differences. Yes, in other Parliaments we may be opposing parties, but within this chamber we are not. No matter how much I may wish it, the SNP is not the sole opposition to this Government, but nor is the Labour party. It is together with all the parties on these benches that we must form an opposition, and in order to be effective, we must oppose, not abstain. So I reach out a genuine hand of friendship which I can only hope will be taken. Let us come together, let us be that opposition, let us be that signpost of a better society.

ANNIE POWELL
(1906–1986)

From a Socialist in Scotland to a Communist in Wales. Annie Powell started off her career as a teacher, but when faced with the poverty children were living in, turned to politics. It was an actress who performed in *Yap Yap Yap* in Swansea, Wales, Alison Lenihan, who found this incredible woman.

After 13 attempts Powell was elected as a Communist councillor for Penygraig in 1955. After over 20 years serving the community, she was appointed Mayor in 1979.

Here is an excerpt from one of her campaign leaflets, which no doubt would have been spoken aloud at the time. It's partly alien, what with the apocalyptic threat of the H-bomb, and partly too familiar for those of us who have lived through austerity since 2010.

Ladies and gentlemen,

It is my privilege to be the Communist Candidate chosen for Rhondda East on this occasion. Peace or war is the main challenge in this General Election, and I am proud to be the first woman to contest this issue in the Rhondda.

The Tories have announced they are producing the Hydrogen Bomb and will use it. The right-wing Labour leaders, to their eternal shame, support them. Famous scientists warn us that the H-Bomb will cause not only a torturing death for millions, but mass poisoning by atomic radiation for children yet unborn. Last time we escaped heavy raids, but with one H-Bomb in South Wales there will be no escape. Death and destruction would come to every street in the Rhondda.

Every day I teach 36 children. They are fine lively youngsters, bigger, stronger and better dressed than ever before. They are reaping the benefit of the big struggles and sacrifices of their parents. It is not Tory rule, but united working-class action which has achieved this.

These young lives are now in terrible danger. Is there a Rhondda mother or father, watching their young children at play, or sleeping peacefully at night, who can bear to think of them dead or maimed for life? This is the dreadful prospect facing the British people and the whole world.

This terrible threat can be defeated. Great as is the power of the H-Bomb, the power of the British people is greater still. The great majority of the people in the world are against it. The Soviet Union and other governments representing 1,400 million people have called for its abolition. Only the governments of the United States, Britain and Western Germany are threatening to use it. I give my solemn pledge to strive with all my might to ensure peace.

All my life I have lived among the people of the Rhondda. I was born in a Welsh-speaking home, trained as a schoolteacher and started my teaching career in Trealaw during the pre-war days of mass unemployment and heart-breaking poverty. My experiences made me burn with indignation, and ever since I have given all my energy to the great struggle of the working class.

In those days when my husband and I were active members of the Methodist Central Hall in Tonypandy and the Trealaw Community House I helped to raise funds to provide the kiddies with boots and clothes and assisted in the mighty campaigns against mass unemployment and the means test. I recognised then it was the Communist Party which was leading the great fight, and my place was in its ranks.

All my adult life I have been an active trade unionist and co-operator and supported every fight of the miners, unemployed, and old-age pensioners. The Communist programme is more in line with the declared policy of the Welsh miners than that of Mr Mainwaring, whose votes in the House of Commons have been contrary to their conference resolutions.

Year in and year out Rhondda mothers and wives perform miracles struggling to make ends meet, bringing up their families and keeping them clothed and in good health. They have to wage this battle in overcrowded houses, badly equipped, and often so damp as to cause a serious threat to good health.

While I have always emphasised that only united action of the workers themselves can make a real change in their conditions, I have been able to assist hundreds of families on their problems of house repairs, pensions and education.

Nothing but the best is good enough for our splendid young people in the Rhondda. We have the right to be proud of our sportsmen, artists, musicians, actors and writers. Our young people need better facilities for education and technical training, playing fields, cycle tracks, covered swimming baths, gymnasia and concert halls.

It is only Communist policy which offers a bright future for our youth in the Rhondda with security of employment through peace, East–West trade and higher living standards.

The greatest debt of all we owe to the old-age pensioners. They should not have to rely on charity. They deserve a pension sufficient to provide them with their needs, and I shall fight for a £3 a week pension for single persons and £5 for married couples.

Rhondda needs an MP who remains true to the principles of the old Labour pioneers. They need someone who fights against the policy of Labour–Toryism. They need an MP who will voice the real opinions of the Welsh miners, of the ordinary men and women of the Rhondda, and who stands for genuine Labour principles.

MARGARET THATCHER

(1925-2013)

THE LADY'S NOT FOR TURNING

In a book full of women with strong, polarising opinions, Thatcher reigns as one of the most divisive figures. Some of my best friends grew up in houses where she was considered a hero. I grew up in a household in the 80s where the name Thatcher was dirt.

Today, when we tour *Yap Yap Yap*, we always end with one of her speeches. In Swansea, in Annie Powell's Wales, you can hear the gasps of incomprehension, bums ready to lift off seats and leave the theatre.

If we really are to stand on the shoulders of giants, to be able to build on the thought leadership of those before us, we cannot cherry pick what ideas we hear. We can absolutely choose who we agree with, but we should be able to listen to those with whom we passionately disagree. How else can you ever hope to persuade anybody of your point of view if you don't have a clue what other people are thinking? And how else are we going to evolve in our ideas, unless we hear or read ideas we've never heard or read before?

One reason I picked this speech for the show and this book is because it contains one of the most famous soundbites from a woman – 'the lady's not for turning'.

And the other reason is that today, in 2019, this speech takes on new meaning, bigger than the lady behind it. This speech sounds kind of familiar. Spookily familar! There was a celebrity, Ronald Reagan, in the White House. Thatcher talks about a debt run up by her predecessors – Labour. Trident is being commissioned for the first time and is just being recommissioned now. The list goes on … . Afghanistan is on the agenda, Russia is seen as the big threat abroad, while the 'the Left wing Orwellian nightmare of Labour' is the threat at home, and to top it off, Thatcher emphasises the UK's commitment to the European Community.

It's 1980.

It's Brighton.

You are one of the UK's biggest political parties.

Ladies and Gentlemen, your (first female) Prime Minister.

Mr Chairman, ladies and gentlemen, most of my Cabinet colleagues have started their speeches of reply by paying very well deserved tributes to their junior Ministers. At Number 10 I have no junior Ministers. There is just Denis and me, and I could not do without him.

In its first 17 months this Government has laid the foundations for recovery. In his first Budget Geoffrey Howe began to restore incentives to stimulate the abilities and inventive genius of our people.

Under Geoffrey's stewardship, Britain has repaid $3,600 million of international debt, debt which had been run up by our predecessors. And we paid quite a lot of it before it was due. This Government thinks about the future.

If spending money like water was the answer to our country's problems, we would have no problems now. If ever a nation has spent, spent, spent and spent again, ours has. Today that dream is over. All of that money has got us nowhere but it still has to come from somewhere. Without a healthy economy we cannot have a healthy society.

To those waiting with bated breath for that favourite media catchphrase, the 'U' turn, I have only one thing to say. 'You turn if you want to. The lady's not for turning.'

I say that not only to you, but to our friends overseas and also to those who are not our friends.

In foreign affairs we have pursued our national interest robustly while remaining alive to the needs and interests of others.

Long before we came into office, and therefore long before the invasion of Afghanistan, I was pointing to the threat from the East. I was accused of scaremongering. But events have more than justified my words.

Soviet Marxism is ideologically, politically and morally bankrupt. But militarily the Soviet Union is a powerful and growing threat.

The British Government are not indifferent to the occupation of Afghanistan. We shall not allow it to be forgotten.

The Soviet Union cannot conduct wars by proxy in South-East Asia and Africa, foment trouble in the Middle East and Caribbean and invade neighbouring countries and still expect to conduct business as usual. That is the message we shall be delivering loud and clear at the meeting of the European Security Conference.

We are acquiring, with the co-operation of the United States Government, the Trident missile system. This will ensure the credibility of our strategic deterrent until the end of the century and beyond, and it was very important for the reputation of Britain abroad that we should keep our independent nuclear deterrent as well as for our citizens here.

In Europe we have shown that it is possible to combine a vigorous defence of our own interests with a deep commitment to the idea and to the ideals of the Community.

With each day it becomes clearer that in the wider world we face darkening horizons, and the war between Iran and Iraq is the latest symptom of a deeper malady. Europe and North America are centres of stability in an increasingly anxious world. The Community and the

Alliance are the guarantee to other countries that democracy and freedom of choice are still possible. They stand for order and the rule of law in an age when disorder and lawlessness are ever more widespread.

The British Government intend to stand by both these great institutions, the European Community and NATO. We will not betray them.

We close our Conference in the aftermath of that sinister Utopia unveiled at Blackpool. Let Labour's Orwellian nightmare of the Left be the spur for us to dedicate with a new urgency our every ounce of energy and moral strength to rebuild the fortunes of this free nation.

If we were to fail, that freedom could be imperilled. So let us resist the blandishments of the faint hearts; let us ignore the howls and threats of the extremists; let us stand together and do our duty, and we shall not fail.

MARGARET SMITH
(1897–1995)
DECLARATION OF CONSCIENCE

Another Margaret, this time on the other side of the pond, and 30 years earlier. Smith followed her husband into politics as a member of the Republican Party (a moderate member), and became the first woman to serve in both houses of the United States Congress.

Smith was the first woman to be placed in nominations for the presidency at a major party convention in 1964, an impressive achievement. I wonder if she thought there would have been a successful woman candidate by 2019!

I picked this speech because it is in part about free speech, about listening to unpopular opinions and people you dislike. But it's also about division, and politics being polarising. Anyone on the left being called a Communist, anyone on the right being called a Fascist. It is remarkably familiar given the situation we find ourselves in today, and Smith has some answers for us.

I think that it is high time for the United States Senate and its members to do some soul-searching – for us to weigh our consciences – on the manner in which we are performing our duty to the people of America – on the manner in which we are using or abusing our individual powers and privileges.

I think that it is high time that we remembered that we have sworn to uphold and defend the Constitution. I think that it is high time that we remembered that the Constitution, as amended, speaks not only of the freedom of speech but also of trial by jury instead of trial by accusation.

Whether it be a criminal prosecution in court or a character prosecution in the Senate, there is little practical distinction when the life of a person has been ruined.

Those of us who shout the loudest about Americanism in making character assassinations are all too frequently those who, by our own words and acts, ignore some of the basic principles of Americanism:

The right to criticise;
The right to hold unpopular beliefs;
The right to protest;
The right of independent thought.

The exercise of these rights should not cost one single American citizen his reputation or his right to a livelihood, nor should he be in danger of losing his reputation or livelihood merely because he happens to know someone who holds unpopular beliefs. Who of us doesn't? Otherwise none of us could call our souls our own. Otherwise thought control would have set in.

The American people are sick and tired of being afraid to speak their minds lest they be politically smeared as 'Communists' or 'Fascists' by their opponents. Freedom of speech is not what it used to be in America. It has been so abused by some that it is not exercised by others.

The American people are sick and tired of seeing innocent people smeared and guilty people whitewashed. But there have been enough proved cases, such as the *Amerasia* case, the Hiss case, the Coplon case, the Gold case, to cause the nationwide distrust and strong suspicion that there may be something to the unproved, sensational accusations.

As a Republican, I say to my colleagues on this side of the aisle that the Republican Party faces a challenge today that is not unlike the challenge that it faced back in Lincoln's day. The Republican Party so successfully met that challenge that it emerged from the Civil War as the champion of a united nation – in addition to being a Party that unrelentingly fought loose spending and loose programmes.

Today our country is being psychologically divided by the confusion and the suspicions that are bred in the United States Senate to spread like cancerous

tentacles of 'know nothing, suspect everything' attitudes.

Today we have a Democratic Administration that has developed a mania for loose spending and loose programmes. History is repeating itself – and the Republican Party again has the opportunity to emerge as the champion of unity and prudence.

The record of the present Democratic Administration has provided us with sufficient campaign issues without the necessity of resorting to political smears. America is rapidly losing its position as leader of the world simply because the Democratic Administration has pitifully failed to provide effective leadership.

The Democratic Administration has completely confused the American people by its daily contradictory grave warnings and optimistic assurances – that show the people that our Democratic Administration has no idea of where it is going.

The Democratic Administration has greatly lost the confidence of the American people by its complacency to the threat of communism here at home and the leak of vital secrets to Russia though key officials of the Democratic Administration. There are enough proved cases to make this point without diluting our criticism with unproved charges.

Surely these are sufficient reasons to make it clear to the American people that it is time for a change and that a Republican victory is necessary to the security of this country. Surely it is clear that this nation will continue to suffer as long as it is governed by the present ineffective Democratic Administration.

Yet to displace it with a Republican regime embracing a philosophy that lacks political integrity or intellectual honesty would prove equally disastrous to this nation. The nation sorely needs a Republican victory. But I don't want to see the Republican Party ride to political victory on the Four Horsemen of Calumny – Fear, Ignorance, Bigotry and Smear.

I doubt if the Republican Party could, simply because I don't believe the American people will uphold any political party that puts political exploitation above national interest. Surely we Republicans aren't that desperate for victory.

I don't want to see the Republican Party win that way. While it might be a fleeting victory for the Republican Party, it would be a more lasting defeat for the American people. Surely it would ultimately be suicide for the Republican Party and the two-party system that has protected our American liberties from the dictatorship of a one-party system.

As members of the Minority Party, we do not have the primary authority to formulate the policy of our Government.

But we do have the responsibility of rendering constructive criticism, of clarifying issues, of allaying fears by acting as responsible citizens.

As a woman, I wonder how the mothers, wives, sisters and daughters feel about the way in which members of their families have been politically mangled in the Senate debate – and I use the word 'debate' advisedly.

As a United States Senator, I am not proud of the way in which the Senate has been made a publicity platform for irresponsible sensationalism. I am not proud of the reckless abandon in which unproved charges have been hurled from this side of the aisle. I am not proud of the obviously staged, undignified counter charges that have been attempted in retaliation from the other side of the aisle.

I don't like the way the Senate has been made a rendezvous for vilification, for selfish political gain at the sacrifice of individual reputations and national unity. I am not proud of the way we smear outsiders from the Floor of the Senate and hide behind the cloak of congressional immunity and still place ourselves beyond criticism on the Floor of the Senate.

As an American, I am shocked at the way Republicans and Democrats alike are playing directly into the Communist design of 'confuse, divide and conquer'. As an American, I don't want a Democratic Administration 'whitewash' or 'cover-up' any more than I want a Republican smear or witch hunt.

As an American, I condemn a Republican 'Fascist' just as much I condemn a Democratic 'Communist'. I condemn a Democrat 'Fascist' just as much as I condemn a Republican 'Communist'. They are equally dangerous to you and me and to our country. As an American, I want to see our nation recapture the strength and unity it once had when we fought the enemy instead of ourselves.

It is with these thoughts that I have drafted what I call a 'Declaration of Conscience'. I am gratified that Senator Tobey, Senator Aiken, Senator Morse, Senator Ives, Senator Thye and Senator Hendrickson have concurred in that declaration and have authorised me to announce their concurrence.

The declaration reads as follows:

1. We are Republicans. But we are Americans first. It is as Americans that we express our concern with the growing confusion that threatens the security and stability of our country. Democrats and Republicans alike have contributed to that confusion.

2. The Democratic Administration has initially created the confusion by its lack of effective leadership, by its contradictory grave warnings and optimistic assurances, by its complacency to the threat of

Communism here at home, by its over-sensitiveness to rightful criticism, by its petty bitterness against its critics.

3. Certain elements of the Republican Party have materially added to this confusion in the hopes of riding the Republican Party to victory through the selfish political exploitation of fear, bigotry, ignorance and intolerance. There are enough mistakes of the Democrats for Republicans to criticise constructively without resorting to political smears.

4. To this extent, Democrats and Republicans alike have unwittingly, but undeniably, played directly into the Communist design of 'confuse, divide and conquer'.

5. It is high time that we stopped thinking politically as Republicans and Democrats about elections and started thinking patriotically as Americans about national security based on individual freedom. It is high time that we all stopped being tools and victims of totalitarian techniques – techniques that, if continued here unchecked, will surely end what we have come to cherish as the American way of life.

CHAPTER 8
REBELS

'Oh Bondage, Up Yours!'
X-Ray Spex

You know that phrase: 'It's easier to ask forgiveness than to get permission'? I'm very much an ask permission kind of person, though I might be asking permission for something a bit odd. Rebels don't ask for permission and don't apologise. The stakes are too high. That's why I love them, and why I hope that if I am ever in a situation where I feel I need to take drastic action, I will be that brave.

Sacheen Littlefeather didn't ask permission from the Oscars in order to make a stand in front of millions, risking her career and upsetting powerful people. Countess Markievicz told Irish women to go out and buy guns instead of backing down against the English. Emmeline Pankhurst went to prison again and again and again. Sophie Scholl paid the ultimate price and was still unrelenting to her captors as they put her to death.

Here's to the rebels. You never know when you might need one.

SACHEEN LITTLEFEATHER

(1946–)

REFUSING AN OSCAR FOR WOUNDED KNEE

There's having allies, and then there's having Marlon Brando as your ally. Actress and activist Littlefeather was supported in her cause by Brando, as he helped give her a platform to millions. When he was expected to win Best Actor at the 1973 Oscars, for his role in *The Godfather*, he boycotted and let Littlefeather go in his place.

Littlefeather wanted to draw attention to a violent standoff between the government and Native Americans at Wounded Knee, where the American Indian Movement were demanding the US government reopen treaty talks.

She was also protesting the portrayal of her people by the film industry. As Brando's win was announced she took to the stage, refusing to take the statuette from presenter Roger Moore, and used the 60 seconds she had to give this speech.

Hello. My name is Sacheen Littlefeather. I'm Apache and I am President of the National Native American Affirmative Image Committee.

I'm representing Marlon Brando this evening and he has asked me to tell you in a very long speech, which I cannot share with you presently because of time, but I will be glad to share with the press afterwards, that he very regretfully cannot accept this very generous award.

And the reasons for this being the treatment of American Indians today by the film industry – excuse me – and on television in movie reruns, and also with recent happenings at Wounded Knee.

I beg at this time that I have not intruded upon this evening and that we will in the future, our hearts and our understandings will meet with love and generosity.

Thank you on behalf of Marlon Brando.

COUNTESS MARKIEVICZ
(1868–1927)
ARM YOURSELVES WITH WEAPONS

Have you heard of this woman? Because I hadn't, not until *Derry Girls* actress and activist Nicola Coughlan joined *Yap Yap Yap* for a show in London and brought this incredible speech with her.

Well, we all should have, not only because she was the first ever woman elected to the British House of Commons – although she never took her seat – but she was also the first woman in the world to hold a cabinet position in the Irish Republic.

The reasons why she's not revered in the same way other political women of her time have been probably have something to do with her having often had a gun in her hand. She was a Nationalist; she wanted the English out of Ireland, and she despised Unionists (those who wanted a United Kingdom), even the Unionist suffragettes. The establishment did not like this revolutionary woman. She would have been considered a terrorist by many.

One person's terrorist is always another person's freedom fighter. While you may disagree with some of her actions, I admire her courage. Markievicz's anger at what she saw as unjust, and her boldness and bravery to be uncompromising, are what made her a danger, but they're also exactly what pushed her to break down barriers blocking women from positions of power. She broke down those barriers by being persuasive, by being a leader, by being able to make a call to arms. That's what she did with this lecture, given to the young women of the National Literary Society in Dublin in 1909.

I take it as a great compliment that so many of you, the rising young women of Ireland, who are distinguishing yourselves every day and coming more and more to the front, should give me this opportunity. We older people look to you with great hopes and a great confidence that in your gradual emancipation you are bringing fresh ideas, fresh energies and above all a great genius for sacrifice into the life of the nation.

Now, I am not going to discuss the subtle psychological question of why it was that so few women in Ireland have been prominent in the national struggle, or try to discover how they lost in the dark ages of persecution the magnificent legacy of Queen Maeve, Fheas, Macha and their other great fighting ancestors. True, several women distinguished themselves on the battlefields of 1798, and we have the women of the *Nation* newspaper, of the Ladies' Land League, also in our own day the few women who have worked their hardest in the Sinn Féin movement and in the Gaelic League, and we have the women who won a battle for Ireland by preventing a wobbly Corporation from presenting King Edward of England with a loyal address.

But for the most part our women, though sincere, steadfast Nationalists at heart, have been content to remain quietly at home, and leave all the fighting and the striving to the men.

Lately things seem to be changing ... so now again a strong tide of liberty seems to be coming towards us, swelling and growing and carrying before it all the outposts that hold women enslaved and bearing them triumphantly into the life of the nation to which they belong.

We are in a very difficult position here, as so many Unionist women would fain [gladly] have us work together with them for the emancipation of their sex and votes – obviously to send a member to Westminster. But I would ask every nationalist woman to pause before she joined a Suffrage Society or Franchise League that did not include in the programme the Freedom of their Nation. A Free Ireland with No Sex Disabilities in her Constitution should be the motto of all Nationalist Women. And a grand motto it is.

Women, from having till very recently stood so far removed from all politics, should be able to formulate a much clearer and more incisive view of the political situation than men.

For a man from the time he is a mere lad is more or less in touch with politics, and has usually the label of some party attached to him, long before he properly understands what it really means ...

Now, here is a chance for our women ... Fix your mind on the ideal of Ireland free, with her women enjoying the full right of citizenship in their own nation, and no one will be able to sidetrack you, and so make use of you to use up the energies of the nation in obtaining all sorts of concessions – concessions too, that for the most part were coming in the natural course of evolution, and were perhaps just hastened a few years by the fierce agitations to obtain them.

If the women of Ireland would organise the movement for buying Irish goods more, they might do a great deal to help their country. If they would make it the fashion to dress in Irish clothes, feed on Irish food – in fact, in this as in everything, live really Irish lives, they would be doing something great, and don't let our clever Irish colleens rest content with doing this individually, but let them go out and speak publicly about it, form leagues, of which 'No English goods' is the war cry ...

I daresay you will think this all very obvious and very dull, but Patriotism and Nationalism and all great things are made up of much that is obvious and dull, and much that in the beginning is small, but that will be found to lead out into fields that are broader and full of interest. You will go out into the world and get elected onto as many public bodies as possible, and by degrees through your exertions no public institution – whether hospital, workhouse, asylum, or any other – and no private house but will be supporting the industries of your country ...

To sum up in a few words what I want the Young Ireland women to remember from me: Regard yourselves as Irish, believe in yourselves as Irish, as units of a nation distinct from England ... and as determined to maintain your distinctiveness and gain your deliverance. Arm yourselves with weapons to fight your nation's cause. Arm your souls with noble and free ideas. Arm your minds with the histories and memories of your country and her martyrs, her language and a knowledge of her arts and her industries ...

EMMELINE PANKHURST
(1858-1928)
FREEDOM OR DEATH

You'll have heard of the Pankhursts, right? This incredible family of women helped lead the suffragette movement. Emmeline was the mother, born in Manchester into a highly politicised family. She founded the Women's Franchise League and later the Women's Social and Political Union with the motto 'Deeds, not Words'.

And their deeds were militant, with Emmeline receiving repeated prison sentences. But then Emmeline was serious about change, and the stakes couldn't be higher. This was about freedom, or death, and it was worth making people feel 'uncomfortable', she told the people of Hartford, Connecticut, in 1913.

I am here as a soldier who has temporarily left the field of battle in order to explain what civil war is like when civil war is waged by women. I am not only here as a soldier temporarily absent from the field at battle; I am here as a person who, according to the law courts of my country, is of no value to the community at all; and I am adjudged because of my life to be a dangerous person, under sentence of penal servitude in a convict prison. I do not look either very like a soldier or very like a convict, and yet I am both.

In England there is a strange manifestation taking place, a new form of hysteria being swept across part of the feminist population of those Isles, and this manifestation takes the shape of irresponsible breaking of windows, burning of letters, general inconvenience to respectable, honest business people who want to attend to their business. It is very irrational, you say: even if these women had sufficient intelligence to understand what they were doing, and really did want the vote, they have adopted very irrational means for getting the vote. 'How are they going to persuade people that they ought to have the vote by breaking their windows?' you say.

We have had to make a great many people very uncomfortable. Now, one woman was arrested on an occasion when a great many windows were broken in London, as a protest against a piece of trickery on the part of the government. Women broke some windows as a protest; they broke a good many shopkeepers' windows; they broke the windows of shopkeepers where they spent most of their money; where they bought their hats and their clothing. They also broke the windows of many of the clubs; the smart clubs in Piccadilly.

One of the clubs was the Guard Club. Well, the ordinary army man is not much in politics, but he very often, because of his aristocratic and social connections, has considerable influence if he would use it. One woman broke the windows of the Guard Club, and when she broke those windows she stood there quietly until the Guard hall porter came out and seized her and held her until the policemen came to take her to prison. A number of the guards came out to see the kind of woman it was who had broken their windows, and they saw there a quiet little woman. She happened to be an actress, a woman who had come into our militant movement because she knew of the difficulties and dangers and temptations of the actress's life, of how badly paid she is, what her private sorrows are and her difficulties, and so she had come into the militant move- ment to get votes for actresses as quickly as possible, so that through the vote they could secure better conditions. Some of the guards – I think men who had never known what it was to earn a living, who knew nothing of the diffi- culties of a man's life, let alone the difficulties of a woman's life – came out, and they said: 'Why did you break our windows? We have done nothing.' She said: 'It is because you have done nothing [that] I have broken your windows.'

The shopkeepers could not understand why we should break the shopkeepers' windows. Why should we alienate the sympathy of the shopkeepers? Well, there is the other side of the question, gentlemen – why should the shopkeep- ers alienate the sympathy of their customers by refusing to help them to get political power? Those women broke shopkeepers' windows, and what was the situation? Just at the beginning of the winter season when all the new winter hats and coats were being shown, the shopkeepers had to barricade all their windows with wood and nobody could see the new winter fashions. Well, there again is an impossible situation. The shopkeeper cannot afford to quarrel with his customers, and we have today far more practical sympathy amongst the shopkeepers of London than we ever had when we were quiet, gentle, ladylike suffragists asking nicely for a vote.

Then there were the men of pleasure, or the business-men who were so busy earning money during the week that all they could think of when the week came to an end was recreation, and the great recreation in England today is playing golf. Everywhere on Saturday you see men streaming away into the country for the weekend to play golf. They so monopolise the golf links that they have made a rule that although the ladies may play golf all the week, the golf links are entirely reserved for men on Saturday and Sunday, and you have this spectacle of the exodus of men from London into the country to fill up the week-end with playing golf. They are not, ladies, putting their heads together thinking how best they can govern the country for you, what good laws they can make for you and for the world: they are there, all of them, getting their health, and I do not blame them for it, at the week-end. Well, we attacked the golf links; we wanted to make them think, and if you had been in London and taken a Sunday paper you would have read, especially if you played golf, with consternation, that all the beautiful greens that had taken years to make had been cut up or destroyed with an acid or made almost impossible to play upon.

I was staying at a little house in the country on a golf links and several times in the course of that Sunday morning I got telephone calls from gentlemen who were prominent members of golf clubs in that vicinity. It so happened that the golf links where I was spending the weekend had not been touched. Those links had been respected because some of the prominent women suffragettes happened to be members of the club, and those women who destroyed the greens – I don't know who they were, but it was no doubt done by women – spared the links where these women, whom they admired and respected, played. Well, then that morning I was rung up over and over again by excited gentlemen who begged that those golf links should be spared, saying: 'I don't know whether your followers know that we are all suffragists, on our committee, we are entirely in favour of woman suffrage.' And I said: 'Well, don't you think you had better tell Mr Asquith so, because if you are suffragists and do nothing, naturally you will only add to the indignation of the women. If you really want your golf links spared you had better intimate to Mr Asquith that you think it is high time he put his principles into practice and gave the women the vote.' There was another gentleman who rang up and said: 'The members of our committee, who are all suffragists, are seriously considering turning all the women members out of the club if this sort of thing goes on.' 'Well,' I said, 'don't you think your greater safety is to keep the women in the club as a sort of insurance policy against anything happening to your links?'

We found that all the fine phrases about freedom and liberty were entirely for male consumption, and that they did not in any way apply to women. When it was said taxation without representation is tyranny, when it was 'taxation of men without representation is tyranny', everybody quite calmly accepted the fact that women had to pay taxes and even were sent to prison if they failed to pay them – quite right. We found that 'government of the people, by the people and for the people', which is also a time-honoured Liberal principle, was again only for male consumption; half of the people were entirely ignored; it was the duty of women to pay their taxes and obey the laws and look as pleasant as they could under the circumstances. In fact, every principle of liberty enunciated in any civilised country on earth, with very few exceptions, was intended entirely for men, and when women tried to force the putting into practice of these principles, for women, then they discovered they had come into a very, very unpleasant situation indeed.

In our civil war people have suffered, but you cannot make omelettes without breaking eggs; you cannot have civil war without damage to something. The great thing is to see that no more damage is done than is absolutely necessary, that you do just as much as will arouse enough feeling to bring about peace, to bring about an honourable peace for the combatants, and that is what we have been doing.

'Put them in prison,' they said, 'that will stop it'. But it didn't stop it. They put women in prison for long terms of imprisonment, for making a nuisance of themselves – that was the expression when they took petitions in their hands to the door of the House of Commons; and they thought that by sending them to prison, giving them a day's imprisonment, would cause them to all settle down again and there would be no further trouble. But it didn't happen so at all: instead of the women giving it up, more women did it, and more and more and more women did it until there were 300 women at a time, who had not broken a single law, only 'made a nuisance of themselves' as the politicians say. Well, then they thought they must go a little further, and so then they began imposing punishments of a very serious kind. The judge who sentenced me last May to three years penal servitude for certain speeches in which I had accepted responsibility for acts of violence done by other women, said that if I could say I was sorry, if I could promise not to do it again, that he would revise the sentence and shorten it, because he admitted that it was a very heavy sentence, especially as the jury recommended me to mercy because of the purity of my motives, and he said he was giving me a determinate sentence, a sentence that would convince me that I would give up my 'evil ways' and would also deter other women from imitating me. But it hadn't that effect at all. So far from it having that effect, more and more women have been doing these things I had incited them to do, and were more determined in doing them: so that the long determinate sentence had no effect in crushing the agitation.

They little know what women are. Women are very slow to rouse, but once they are aroused, once they are determined, nothing on earth and nothing in heaven will make women give way; it is impossible.

So here am I. I come in the intervals of prison appearance: I come after having been four times imprisoned under the 'Cat and Mouse Act', probably going back to be re-arrested as soon as I set my foot on British soil. I come to ask you to help to win this fight. If we win it, this hardest of all fights, then, to be sure, in the future it is going to be made easier for women all over the world to win their fight when their time comes.

SOPHIE SCHOLL

(1921–1943)

LAST WORDS

Scholl was a student and a White Rose anti-Nazi activist in Germany. Alongside her older brother Hans, Sophie was found guilty of distributing anti-war pamphlets and sentenced to death by guillotine at the age of 21.

The leaflet was smuggled out of Germany and reprinted as 'The Manifesto of the Students of Munich', and millions of copies were air dropped over Germany by Allied troops.

As Scholl was taken to her death she said ...

How can we expect righteousness to prevail when there is hardly anyone willing to give himself up individually to a righteous cause?

Such a fine, sunny day, and I have to go, but what does my death matter, if through us thousands of people are awakened and stirred to action?

CHAPTER 9

FREEDOM

'Freeing yourself was one thing,
claiming ownership of that freed
self was another.'
Toni Morrison

There's nothing more life affirming than quitting a job. Letting
the door slam behind you as you strut off with the wind in your
hair. As every bit of office politics, photocopier etiquette and
your boss's love of Gantt charts just falls away from your
shoulders. It is bliss. Sweet freedom.

I remember the first time I quit a job. It was by far the most
glamorous job I'd ever had (previous to that, working at Boots
had held the title). I was a receptionist at a film company. I could
smoke at my desk, got to watch pop videos all day, and I could
order from the stationery catalogue whenever I wanted, result-
ing in my receiving a lot of the complimentary chocolates you
get when you bulk buy envelopes.

I'd told my boss that I wanted to be a director. He said that
wasn't going to happen. That women go into producer roles

and men become directors. This was 2002, and this was bare-faced sexism. So I decided to quit. I went up to the boss and told him I was leaving, that I had another job and here was my two weeks' notice. He was furious. 'You don't tell me when you leave, I tell you when you leave,' he said. Er, nope! And I was off.

When I'm asked what this book is about, there are some pretty obvious answers. Women's speeches. Yup, definitely about that. Feminism. Absolutely, this book is jam-packed full of feminism. Women's history. Smatterings of that too. But if I had to pick one thing, one word, this book is about freedom.

Freedom to talk, love, move, be. Freedom to take part in politics, to debate, to rebel. Freedom to dream. Even with all our privileges, it can be hard to think of ourselves as free, because it's so easy to feel stuck. Stuck in a shitty financial situation. Stuck in a crappy relationship. Stuck in a body that doesn't do what you want.

Freedom is hard. Freedom requires risk and responsibility. So if we have it, we must exercise it, so we don't lose it.

Whether that's freedom through technology as Joanne O'Riordan found. Allowing yourself to truly express yourself in spite of the reaction of others as Paula Stone Williams describes. Or fighting for all our human rights like Eleanor Roosevelt. We end this chapter with Nora Ephron challenging us, saying that we no longer have excuses; we have all the tools we need to be free and we need to be vigilant.

JOANNE O'RIORDAN

(1996–)

GIRLS IN TECHNOLOGY

O'Riordan is an Irish sports journalist from Millstreet in Cork, and one of just a handful of people in the world born with Tetra-amelia syndrome.

In 2012, in the week of her 16th birthday she was invited to New York to speak at the International Telecommunication Union's conference 'Girls in Technology'. This is what she said about how technology had given her freedom, as she challenged the audience to build her a robot.

As you can see I was born without my limbs, but my motto in life is 'No Limbs, No Limits'. The disability I have is known as Tetra-amelia syndrome and it is one of the rarest conditions known to us. I believe there are only seven people in the world living with this physical form and furthermore there is no medical explanation as to why I was born this way.

However, my family and I have never allowed it to hold me back.

From an early age I have always relied on the use of technology to help advance my abilities. Be this in moving or communicating, I developed an understanding of what I could achieve with technology from a young age.

I use technology in all aspects of my life, be it at home, in school or through the wider medium of interacting with others. My parents have told me that when I was one I first began to explore the use of technology with our old computer. I figured out how to use this software by simply moving my 'hand' and chin at a faster speed. Today I can type 36 words a minute and, for someone with no limbs, I think that's an incredible achievement in itself.

The computer allowed me to play and follow certain games, which in turn helped me to learn my ABC, maths and small words such as 'cat' and 'dog'. Needless to say, I'm a fiercely independent person, but when I was born, the technology that was there then was not as advanced as the technology we have now.

All my young life I've struggled and overcome barriers. I've surprised doctors, strangers, friends and even my own family by what I have achieved.

I must admit I'm always finding new ways or methods that would allow me to be the same as any other person. There is no such thing as 'normal' in my vocabulary. When I started school I, like all the other children, used my hand to write. I did this by putting my pen in between my shoulder and chin and, as you can imagine, this was an enormous challenge for me, but I overcame the obstacle. I have always been breaking down barriers and overcoming obstacles. I do not look at the word 'impossible' and see it as impossible.

I look at that word and my life and say I'm possible! Technology has made me even more determined to achieve a better standard and quality of life. I always think, if I can do this now, what would I achieve in the future?

Technology, as we know, is ever-advancing, and my question was soon answered when, at the age of seven, I started to develop a spinal condition known as scoliosis. This is a curvature of the spine. Unfortunately, this meant that I was not able to continue to write as I did and I had to find a new way of learning and developing my educational potential.

I'm very lucky that I have the support of my family, as they have never allowed anyone to hold me back. They have done everything in their power to ensure that I would not lose out on my education, and technology was key in helping me.

A system was set up which allows my schoolbooks to be put onto CDs. This in turn enables me to do all my work through a computer.

Nobody in Ireland has availed [themselves] of this technology and I was extremely lucky to have a woman by the name of Christine O'Mahony helping me to make the process much easier. It took months to get the format right, but when she did my life ultimately changed.

I now discovered that with one flick of my hand I was able to do all the things my other friends were doing with their fingers. I was able to be as good as them, if not better. My quality of life has changed dramatically since I started using technology and only the other day I told my mother that technology is the limb I never had.

I can use my mobile phone, send texts, tweets, update my Facebook, play my PlayStation, Nintendo DS, iPad, iPod, and laptop; without Microsoft, Adobe and Apple in my life I would not be doing and achieving my full potential. In fact I think my life would be quite different to what it is now. Believe it or not, I simply use my upper and bottom lip, chin, nose and hand to work most if not all these systems.

Technology has opened up a world of possibilities, through which I have excelled in both my education and social environment around me.

It is fair to say that I have been given the opportunities to grow, learn and adapt my lifestyle in a way that helps me, but I also know there are children and adults out there all over the world who do not have the same chances in life as I do.

I'm asking the Girls in Technology who are here today and who are the leading women within their field to start doing what I do, in my life: 'Think outside the box.' Think of ways and means that you can make technology more accessible to those who really need it because let's face it, we all know women are better than men at most things, so why not technology too?

It is my wish and it's my challenge to you and to others out there to build me a robot.

Yes, that's right: a robot! It sounds almost insane, but as a child and even today I've always wanted and would love to have a robot.

The main thing the robot would be doing is picking up the objects I drop, such as a pen, knife, fork and/or my phone.

This robot would become my hands and legs. So, for example, if I was in the sitting room and I needed something from the kitchen, I would love for that robot to get me what I needed. I mean – to be fair – when you're lazy and sitting down, most of you use a remote control because you're too lazy to get up and manually switch the TV over – and trust me, that is lazy. So why can't I have a robot?

Call it crazy, call it insane, call it what you like – but the challenges I face every day get bigger and far greater to overcome. I know I can overcome these challenges but I need your help.

I can't rely on my parents, my brothers, sister and others all my life. Can I? Certainly not, and I don't want to!

I want to live an independent life just like you. I don't want to live in the shadow of others because I want to make my own journey in life and I know if I'm given that chance, I can and will succeed. I know that there must be someone out there in the world who can do something like this to make life much easier. It would not just help me, but indeed others who are in similar situations. Life is about living and let's face it ladies, technology is not just a way of life, it's a way of living!

And just because I have no limbs does not mean I will be limited. And neither should you!

PAULA STONE WILLIAMS
(1951–)
WHAT I'VE LEARNED

The Reverend Dr Williams is the pastor at Left Hand Church in Longmont, Colorado, and an LGBTQ activist and speaker. Williams came out as a transgender woman in 2012 and lost all her jobs and some of her closest relationships.

In this viral TED Talk, Williams speaks about how she now realises more than ever what male privilege is, and she wonders about what other privileges she, and all of us, still do not fully understand.

Williams sacrificed some of the freedoms associated with male privilege for authenticity, and reveals her own 93-year-old father finally did what we all need to do in order to let each other be free: 'whatever it takes to honour the journey of another'.

I was the CEO of a large religious non-profit, the host of a national television show. I preached in mega churches. I was a successful, well-educated, white American male. The poet and mystic Thomas Merton said, 'It's a difficult thing to climb to the top of the ladder of success only to realise when you get there that your ladder has been leaning against the wrong wall.'

I knew from the time I was three or four years of age I was transgender. In my naivety, I thought I got to choose. I thought a gender fairy would arrive and say, 'OK, the time has come!' But alas, no gender fairy arrived, so I just lived my life. I didn't hate being a boy. I just knew I wasn't one. I went to college, got married, had kids, built a career, but the call towards authenticity has all the subtlety of a smoke alarm. And eventually decisions have to be made.

So I came out as transgender and I lost all of my jobs. I had never had a bad review, and I lost every single job. In 21 states, you can't be fired for being transgender, but in all 50, you can be fired if you're transgender and you work for a religious corporation. Good to know! It's not easy being a transgender woman.

People sometimes ask, 'Do you feel 100% like a woman?' And I say, 'Well, if you've talked to one transgender person, you've talked to exactly one transgender person. I can't speak for anybody else.' I feel 100% like a transgender woman. There are things a cisgender woman knows I will never know. That said, I am learning a lot about what it means to be a female, and I am learning a lot about my former gender. I have the unique experience of having lived life on both sides – and I'm here to tell you the differences are massive.

There is no way a well-educated white male can understand how much the culture is tilted in his favour. There's no way he can understand it because it's all he's ever known, and all he ever will know. And conversely, there's no way that a woman can understand the full import of that because being a female is all she's ever known. She might have an inkling that she's working twice as hard for half as much, but she has no idea how much harder it is for her than it is for the guy in the Brooks Brothers jacket in the office across the hall. I know! I was that guy! And I thought I was one of the good guys, sensitive to women, egalitarian.

Then came the first time I ever flew as a female. Now, I've flown over 2.3 million miles with American Airlines. I know my way around an airplane. And American was great through my transition, but that does not mean their passengers were. The first time I flew as Paula, I was going from Denver to Charlotte, and I got on the plane and there was stuff in my seat. So I picked it up to put my stuff down, and a guy said, 'That's my stuff.' I said, 'OK, but it's in my seat. So I'll just hold it for you until you find your seat, and then I'll give it to you.' He said, 'Lady, that is my seat!' I said, 'Actually, it's not. It's my seat. 1D, 1D. But I'll be glad to hold your stuff until you find your seat.' He said, 'What do I have to tell you? That is my seat!' I said, 'Yeah, it's not.'

At which point the guy behind me said, 'Lady, would you take your effing argument elsewhere so I can get in the airplane?' I was absolutely stunned! I had never been treated like that as a male. I would have said, 'I believe that's my seat', and the guy immediately would have looked at his boarding pass and said, 'Oh, I'm sorry.' I know that because it happened all the time!

The flight attendant took our boarding passes. She said to the guy, 'Sir, you're in 1C. She's in 1D.' I put his stuff down in 1C, he said not one single word, and of course you know who was next to me in 1E. Mr 'would you take your effing argument elsewhere'. So, my friend Karen, who works for American, came on the plane to give the pilot his paperwork. She left and waved goodbye.

When I got to Charlotte, she called me. She said, 'Paula, what happened? You were as white as a sheet!' I told her and she said, 'Yeah. Welcome to the world of women!' Now, the truth is I will not live long enough to lose my male privilege. I brought it with me when I transitioned. A lot of decades of being a man. But that doesn't mean I don't see my power diminishing.

What can you do? You can believe us when we tell you that we might, we might have equality, but we do not have equity. It is not a level playing field, it never has been. You can be a part of the solution by elevating us to equal footing. You uniquely have that power. And to all of us, do you know who I think about a lot? I think about my brown-skinned daughter and my brown-skinned daughter-in-law. What do they know that I'm clueless about? What do any of us really know about the shoes in which we have never walked? It's hard being a woman, it's hard being a transgender woman.

Would I do it all again? Of course I would, because the call towards authenticity is sacred, it's holy, it's for the greater good.

For 45 years, my father was a fundamentalist pastor. My mother is even more conservative. When I came out as transgender, they rejected me. I thought I would never speak to them again.

Last January, I took a chance and called my dad on his birthday, and he took my call. We talked for about a half hour, and about a month later, I asked if I could come for a visit, and they said yes. And last spring, I had a delightfully redemptive three-hour visit with them. I've met with them twice since. But that day, towards the end of the conversation, that first day, my father said a number of precious things. As I stood to go, he said, 'Paula'. He called me Paula. He said, 'Paula, I don't understand this, but I am willing to try.' My father is 93 years old, and he's willing to try. What more could I ask? I hugged him so tightly. One man willing to give up his power because he knew what he knew, that he loved his child, and he was willing to do whatever it takes to honour the journey of another. Thank you.

ELEANOR ROOSEVELT
(1884–1962)
DECLARATION OF HUMAN RIGHTS

Roosevelt has to be one of the most quote-worthy women in history. She's a one-woman historical inspo-gram meme maker:

- No one can make you feel inferior without your consent.
- Great minds discuss ideas; average minds discuss events; small minds discuss people.
- Women are like teabags. You don't know how strong they are until you put them in hot water.

She was a very controversial First Lady, especially as she was so outspoken on civil rights. But she wouldn't stop communicating. She was the first First Lady to write a column, host a radio show and speak at conventions.

Beyond all of this though, Roosevelt became the chair of the United Nations Human Rights Commission, which was to become a huge part of her legacy, and why she would become known as 'First Lady of the World'. Because in 1948, Roosevelt helped enact the first ever Declaration of Human Rights.

We stand today at the threshold of a great event both in the life of the United Nations and in the life of mankind.

This Universal Declaration of Human Rights may well become the international Magna Carta of all men everywhere.

We hope its proclamation by the General Assembly will be an event comparable to the proclamation of the Declaration of the Rights of Man by the French people in 1789, the adoption of the Bill of Rights by the people of the United States and the adoption of comparable declarations at different times in other countries.

At a time when there are so many issues on which we find it difficult to reach a common basis of agreement, it is a significant fact that 58 states have found such a large measure of agreement in the complex field of human rights. This must be taken as testimony of our common aspiration first voiced in the Charter of the United Nations to lift men everywhere to a higher standard of life and to a greater enjoyment of freedom. Man's desire for peace lies behind this Declaration. The realisation that the flagrant violation of human rights by Nazi and Fascist countries sowed the seeds of the last World War has supplied the impetus for the work which brings us to the moment of achievement here today.

In a recent speech in Canada, Gladstone Murray said:

The central fact is that man is fundamentally a moral being. That the light we have is imperfect does not matter so long as we are always trying to improve it ... we are equal in sharing the moral freedom that distinguishes us as men. Man's status makes each individual an end in himself. No man is by nature simply the servant of the state or of another man ... the ideal and fact of freedom – and not technology – are the true distinguishing marks of our civilisation.

This Declaration is based upon the spiritual fact that man must have freedom in which to develop his full stature and through common effort to raise the level of human dignity. We have much to do to fully achieve and to assure the rights set forth in this Declaration. But having them put before us with the moral backing of 58 nations will be a great step forward.

As we here bring to fruition our labours on this Declaration of Human Rights, we must at the same time re-dedicate ourselves to the unfinished task which lies before us. We can now move on with new courage and inspiration to the completion of an international covenant on human rights and of measures for the implementation of human rights.

In conclusion, I feel that I cannot do better than to repeat the call to action by Secretary Marshall in his opening statement to this Assembly:

Let this third regular session of the General Assembly approve by an overwhelming majority the Declaration of Human Rights as a standard of conduct for all; and let us, as Members of the United Nations, conscious of our own shortcomings and imperfections, join our effort in good faith to live up to this high standard.

NORA EPHRON
(1941–2012)
COMMENCEMENT SPEECH

Ephron wrote the most famous fake orgasm scene in history, in *When Harry Met Sally*, and one of the funniest lines in film history: 'I'll have what she's having.' She was a multi award-winning writer and filmmaker.

Like Hillary Rodham Clinton, she also made a commencement speech at Wellesley, but many years later, in 1996. The message she had for the students: you have no excuse, you have everything you need to succeed, don't rely on the freedoms you have, protect them, annnnnd … make a little trouble.

I want to tell you a little bit about my class, the class of 1962. When we came to Wellesley in the fall of 1958, there was an article in the *Harvard Crimson* about the women's colleges, one of those stupid mean little articles full of stereotypes. We were girls then, by the way, Wellesley girls. How long ago was it? It was so long ago that while I was here, Wellesley actually threw six young women out for lesbianism. It was so long ago that we had curfews. It was so long ago that if you had a boy in your room, you had to leave the door open six inches, and if you closed the door you had to put a sock on the doorknob. In my class of, I don't know, maybe 375 young women, there were six

Asians and five Blacks. There was a strict quota on the number of Jews. Tuition was $2,000 a year and in my junior year it was raised to $2,250 and my parents practically had a heart attack.

How long ago? If you needed an abortion, you drove to a gas station in Union, New Jersey, with $500 in cash in an envelope and you were taken, blindfolded, to a motel room and operated on without an anaesthetic. On the lighter side, and as you no doubt read in the *New York Times* magazine, and were flabbergasted to learn, there were the posture pictures. We not only took off most of our clothes to have our posture pictures taken, we took them off without ever even thinking, this is weird, why are we doing this?

Anyway, as I was saying, the *Crimson* had this snippy article which said that Wellesley was a school for tunicata – tunicata apparently being small fish who spend the first part of their lives frantically swimming around the ocean floor exploring their environment, and the second part of their lives just lying there breeding. It was mean and snippy, but it had the horrible ring of truth. It was one of those do-not-ask-for-whom-the-bell-tolls things, and it burned itself into our brains. Years later, at my 25th reunion, one of my classmates mentioned it and everyone remembered what tunicata were, word for word.

My class went to college in the era when you got a Master's degree in teaching because it was 'something to fall back on' in the worst-case scenario, the worst-case scenario being that no one married you and you actually had to go to work. As this same classmate said at our reunion, 'Our education was a dress rehearsal for a life we never led.' Isn't that the saddest line? We weren't meant to have futures, we were meant to marry them. We weren't meant to have politics, or careers that mattered, or opinions, or lives; we were meant to marry them. If you wanted to be an architect, you married an architect.

Many of my classmates did exactly what they were supposed to when they graduated from Wellesley, and some of them, by the way, lived happily ever after. But many of them didn't. All sorts of things happened that no one expected. They needed money so they had to work. They got divorced so they had to work. They were bored witless so they had to work. The women's movement came along and made harsh value judgments about their lives – judgments that caught them by surprise, because they were doing what they were supposed to be doing, weren't they? The rules had changed, they were caught in some kind of strange time warp. They had never intended to be the heroines of their own lives, they'd intended to be – what? First Ladies, I guess, first ladies in the lives of big men. They ended up feeling like victims. They ended up, and this is really sad, thinking that their years in college were the best years of their lives.

Why am I telling you this? It was a long time ago, right? Things have changed, haven't they? Yes, they have. But I mention it because I want to remind you of the undertow, of the specific gravity. American society has a remarkable ability to resist change, or to take whatever change has taken place and attempt to make it go away.

What I'm saying is, don't delude yourself that the powerful cultural values that wrecked the lives of so many of my classmates have vanished from the earth. Don't let the *New York Times* article about the brilliant success of Wellesley graduates in the business world fool you – there's still a glass ceiling. Don't let the number of women in the work force trick you – there are still lots of magazines devoted almost exclusively to making perfect casseroles and turning various things into tents.

Don't underestimate how much antagonism there is towards women and how many people wish we could turn the clock back. One of the things people always say to you if you get upset is 'don't take it personally' but listen hard to what's going on and, please, I beg you, take it personally.

Understand: Every attack on Hillary Clinton for not knowing her place is an attack on you. Underneath almost all

those attacks are the words: Get back, get back to where you once belonged.

Above all, be the heroine of your life, not the victim. Because you don't have the alibi my class had. This is one of the great achievements and mixed blessings you inherit: Unlike us, you can't say nobody told you there were other options. Your education is a dress rehearsal for a life that is yours to lead. Twenty-five years from now, you won't have as easy a time making excuses as my class did. You won't be able to blame the Deans, or the culture, or anyone else: you will have no one to blame but yourselves. Whoa.

Whatever you choose, however many roads you travel, I hope that you choose not to be a lady. I hope you will find some way to break the rules and make a little trouble out there. And I also hope that you will choose to make some of that trouble on behalf of women. Thank you. Good luck. The first act of your life is over. Welcome to the best years of your lives.

CHAPTER 10
UTOPIA

'It isn't elsewhere
It, it's here.'
Björk, *Utopia*

So then, what's your vision? If you were to stand in front of everyone at work or in your town centre, or send it out on a YouTube video to the whole world, what imagined world would you conjure up for us all to live in? Whether you're a comedian, a politician, academic, receptionist, brutal warrior, poet or you work in Boots – what would you change?

Visionaries help us imagine and plan our future. They envision a new, better world, and they tell us about it. They rouse us from the sleepy status quo and help us figure out what to do next. They bring us together and make the impossible seem possible, and often face audiences who don't welcome their inconvenient ideas.

Like Charlotte Church, standing up in front of a room of teachers who know her best as a singer, sharing her vision of the education of the future, saying we should listen to the children. Like Greta Thunberg, the 16-year-old environmentalist, who stood in front of the very people who should have already taken action and shamed them into committing to doing something about our impending environmental catastrophe.

Visionaries like Dame Anita Roddick, who told the International Forum on Globalisation we need a 'revolution of kind business', and Baroness Bertha von Suttner, who explained to the UN why peace is not just some utopian dream.

Neuroscientist and artificial intelligence expert Vivienne Ming shows us a future where tech enables greater human potential. And finally, Mary Wollstonecraft offers up the idea, a dream, that women should be allowed to fill their human potential and not be treated as slaves. Every one of these women offers a new way of thinking to their time and place, a new way of living and, most importantly, hope.

CHARLOTTE CHURCH

(1986–)

EDUCATION

Singer, writer, actress, presenter and activist, the phenomenal Church has now added educationalist to her CV. She has always used her voice though. From singing to speaking at marches, from testifying at the Leveson enquiry to interviewing guests on her own TV show. She could easily have chosen not to go into activism, but she is an outspoken woman.

Born and bred in Wales, she was 'discovered' as a child singer and became an international singing success, selling over 10 million records. Her childhood was extraordinary, with her meeting everyone from the Pope to Elton John and sitting her GCSEs in the White House.

Church is now in the process of building her own school. Here she took to the stage at the SSAT's National Conference in 2018, a room filled with teachers and education experts, to share her vision of the future of education.

My education was very weird and some people think this should disqualify me from holding an opinion on what a normal education should be. But I've developed somewhat of a reputation for being far from shy when it comes to expressing an opinion.

I can set up a school, not in competition with the state system, in collaboration, but free from the demands of the state. Not some middle-class cutesy private school, but a school that does not ask for fees yet provides an education that is fit for the future. A school that funds itself. A school that starts at three and carries on till, I don't know ... 14? 18? 23? I can set up a school that is first a school, and second a centre for education research, that can offer its findings back to the state system. This school can be a trailblazer, and it can do things that fail, and it will answer to nobody but the pupils. New models of learning will live or die in the classroom, not have the life squeezed out of them before they even get there. It will be hard, but from the depths of my being I will drag it into existence.

I admit that I am pretty nervous coming out here today. This is a room full of people whose job I have the utmost respect for and I know it's as hard as it's ever been. For that you have all my admiration. It might sound a bit over-blown, I can think of few things more noble than choosing to educate, and to care about it enough to attend conferences on education, I salute you. The last thing I want to do is to tell you how to do your jobs. I am totally unqualified to do so, and besides, you would no doubt firmly but politely deathstare me off the stage in a matter of seconds, as is the secret power of all head teachers.

What I'm here to say is that what is being required of you is unsustainable, that the circumstances are likely to only get worse, that we need the freedom of pure imagination and the freedom to apply our findings now. I'm not asking you to change the way you are running your schools. I'm asking to stand with you in support of a positive change to the whole education system. Curriculum, architecture, culture, the hardware if you will. A change that follows academic research, rejects the conservative apocrypha of what education should be and understands that children are people who deserve respect, that learning is an active process, that neurotically examining young people and making examinations the primary focus of their education is nothing but a distraction for students and fundamentally fails to assess anything of value, that keeping developing minds from their passions and tasking them with exercises that have little to no relevance to their lives is taking away their natural propensity to learn.

But most importantly we need to stop seeing childhood as a preparation for adulthood. For generations we have attempted to use education to hammer young people into shapes that the indifferent system can recognise. We put the pressure of success directly upon teachers' wages, as if existential terror is a useful motivator. How do we encourage creativity in the classroom? Perhaps allowing students to be themselves and follow their passions would help.

Maybe removing the coldblooded demands upon teachers, that they cajole their pupils to an arbitrary level of achievement within the gaze of some aloof God-robot, to the detriment of those pupils' other skills, maybe that would encourage creativity within the classroom.

...

The future is coming, and the robots are after the white-collar jobs. Soon the mid-management pencil-pusher occupations that were the staple of middle-class professions in the 20th century will be taken by artificial intelligence. In a capitalist system, why would a company pay five people salaries to work admin in rented office space, when one computer could do that work more efficiently in a much smaller space? Our postal workers will soon be drones, our factory production lines are already upturned millipedes with robotic arms.

Is there anything a human can do, that couldn't be done better by a machine? Of course: anything that requires creativity and, actually, empathy. We don't know what the future job market will look like, but we can be pretty certain that those two qualities will be high up on employers, wish lists. If the job market of the last 20 years can be defined as a period of overwork, not enough time, with people cramming information and striving and struggling to be as efficient as humanly possible and then beyond, the next era is likely to require workers with a knack for invention, with the ability to think laterally, collaborative and curious, adaptable and able to take initiative. These are the jobs your students will be applying for.

Skills are the most important thing anybody can walk away from their education with. Everybody can look back at their own schooling and point to something they had to learn which had no relevance to them then and has no relevance to them now. The content of a lesson is far less important than the process. So if the process is content driven then for most students it is a waste of time.

The nitrogen cycle is not exciting. Unless of course the student can see a reason for learning it. Unless they are given a motive for learning it. Unless the lesson is driven by necessity. Neuroscience tells us that we are geared towards learning about the things that matter to us. We learn about what we care about. Without that caring, learning becomes dry and aimless.

Imagination is a response to that need to know; to explore; to get better at the things that fire you up. If we don't respond to the changing world then why not just replace teachers with robots? Why not rely solely on tech to inform the next generation? Well, probably because robots don't have souls, and humans need humans. We are programmed to connect with each other, and this need is as important as water or air. We can see it all around in deteriorating mental health. With more distractions, technology, social media, people are becoming more socially isolated.

Human teachers are always going to be better than tech, as long as they are allowed to show their humanity.

Autonomy within community nurtures necessity. The ringing of bells to mark the end of a lesson removes autonomy. For some students in some classes the bell comes as a blessed relief. For others it marks a brutal end to their allotted time of exploration for their passion. If a young person is showing a passion for something, whether that be an art project or a science experiment, aren't we getting in the way of their learning by insisting that they stop what they're doing and go to another class where they might sit bored, mess around, get into trouble? By the time teenagers are looking at GCSEs some of them already know what they're passionate about.

Of course she is not every pupil. But every pupil has different needs and a 'one size fits all' approach is blatantly inadequate. The philosophy being pushed by people like Nick Gibb, that children, especially those from disadvantaged backgrounds, need to learn rigour and compliance, is frankly insulting and dehumanising to young people, and most importantly will often create the exact opposite of its intention. Of the carrot and the stick, the stick can work in creating uniformity, in the short term. But the psychological effects are unquestionable. Fear and oppression are not things that we would tolerate as adults. We recognise them as wholly negative forces in wider society and yet some will say they are the best way to educate our kids. I say more carrots please. Let's fill our schools with carrots.

...

What I've been talking about today are not new ideas. Jane and Michael's mother, Mrs Banks, the most visible suffragette of the 20th century, would have had a lot to say about education had she been hobnobbing with Emmeline Pankhurst, who set up a Montessori adoption home, or Margaret McMillan, who contributed to the New Ideals In Education Act of 1918.

Over a hundred years earlier, Mary Wollstonecraft and her husband William Godwin were writing about the need to raise children within a culture of rights, liberty and equality. The fact that their ideas are now backed up by a metric tonne of research studies would probably be of little satisfaction to them, seeing as those ideas have been ignored so constantly in the preference for blinkered tradition.

Throughout time the suggestion of change has been barked down as readily as climate warnings. Except that now there is a cowed silence, an acceptance that nothing can be done. Bullshit. If the main reason for not changing the system is money, then I say that is not good enough. I've really tried to keep politics out of this speech, but to do that would be to ignore the greatest obstacle to education reform. At the beginning of this I talked about what change will cost us. Well, it's going to cost a great deal more money than schools are getting at the moment. And that cost should not be negotiable.

We need to start looking at education as economically transformative. It can be looked at as a simple input and output of cash. If we spend on education now, then school leavers in 10 years' time will be more economically prosperous. Fewer will need to use the benefit systems, or require mental health treatment, or physical health treatment. It would mean that the next generation of parents are more active in their children's education.

Vic Goddard, the head of Passmores Academy in Hounslow, one of the most dedicated people I have ever met, says that the reason he has stuck with that school, even though sometimes it's really hard due to the abject poverty of the area, is so he can see his students return as parents with a greater sense of responsibility for their children than theirs did, despite their economic prospects. He's in it for the long game, to see societal change. To provoke economic change. Squeezing public systems to pay off a deficit is ludicrously short-sighted economically. Of course the only result of the squeeze will be greater demand upon those systems.

This idea that we're saving for the future, 'fixing the roof while the sun shines', is such infuriating crap. You're stealing from children to fix the roof. You are stealing from the future. So this system where the government decides on a budget and tells schools to get on with it needs to be flipped on its head. Instead, schools should be deciding what they need to run, how much it is going to cost to educate each student (as Eton and Harrow do) and sending the government a bill. That's what weapons manufacturers do. The last thing we should be saving money on is education, even after health care. Children are the seeds of our economic future. What in God's name are we doing cutting costs around their nourishment?!

I hope that you won't walk away from this thinking I am just an idealist. I mean, of course I am, but without ideals there is no direction, nothing to aim for. We should dream and dream big.

I know I'm not in your shoes, and I don't yet fully understand the complexities that you have to deal with: so many different children from so many walks of life. But I know that the best way we can fix the problems in society, all problems for all of us, is to listen and be heard and to be understood and to ask for somebody to help us find and facilitate what's important; what changes should be made. Let me reiterate that I have nothing but absolute respect and love for you and the superhuman efforts that you all go to to make your schools places of kindness and respect, and I want you to know that I am with you. I'd love it if you could be with me.

GRETA THUNBERG

(2003–)

YOU DID NOT ACT IN TIME

If there were a voice for 2019, it would be Thunberg's. Nominated for the Nobel Peace Prize for her activism at age 16, this Swedish environmental campaigner has captured the world's imagination. This same year she has been on the front cover of *Time* magazine and named the most important woman of the year in Sweden.

Thunberg has Asperger syndrome and selective mutism. She has said that they both are an advantage in that she sees things in 'black and white' and only speaks when it is needed.

In April 2019 she came to London and spoke to MPs, and delivered not just a vision, but a warning on behalf of future generations. What would you say if for a moment you became a poster child politicians queued up to listen to?

My name is Greta Thunberg. I am 16 years old. I come from Sweden. And I speak on behalf of future generations.

I know many of you don't want to listen to us. You say we are just children. But we're only repeating the message of the united climate science.

Many of you appear concerned that we are wasting valuable lesson time, but I assure you we will go back to school the moment you start listening to science and give us a future. Is that really too much to ask?

In the year 2030 I will be 26 years old. My little sister Beata will be 23. Just like many of your own children or grandchildren. That is a great age, we have been told. When you have all of your life ahead of you. But I am not so sure it will be that great for us.

I was fortunate to be born in a time and place where everyone told us to dream big; I could become whatever I wanted to. I could live wherever I wanted to. People like me had everything we needed and more. Things our grandparents could not even dream of. We had everything we could ever wish for and yet now we may have nothing.

Now we probably don't even have a future any more.

Because that future was sold so that a small number of people could make unimaginable amounts of money. It was stolen from us every time you said that the sky was the limit, and that you only live once.

You lied to us. You gave us false hope. You told us that the future was something to look forward to. And the saddest thing is that most children are not even aware of the fate that awaits us. We will not understand it until it's too late. And yet we are the lucky ones. Those who will be affected the hardest are already suffering the consequences. But their voices are not heard.

Is my microphone on? Can you hear me?

Around the year 2030, 10 years 252 days and 10 hours away from now, we will be in a position where we set off an irreversible chain reaction beyond human control, that will most likely lead to the end of our civilisation as we know it. That is unless in that time, permanent and unprecedented changes in all aspects of society have taken place, including a reduction of CO_2 emissions by at least 50%.

And please note that these calculations are depending on inventions that have not yet been invented at scale, inventions that are supposed to clear the atmosphere of astronomical amounts of carbon dioxide.

Furthermore, these calculations do not include unforeseen tipping points and feedback loops like the extremely powerful methane gas escaping from rapidly thawing arctic permafrost.

Nor do these scientific calculations include already locked-in warming hidden by toxic air pollution. Nor the aspect of equity – or climate justice – clearly stated throughout the Paris agreement, which is absolutely necessary to make it work on a global scale.

We must also bear in mind that these are just calculations. Estimations. That means that these 'points of no return' may occur a bit sooner or later than 2030. No one can know for sure. We can, however, be certain that they will occur approximately in these timeframes, because these calculations are not opinions or wild guesses.

These projections are backed up by scientific facts, concluded by all nations through the IPCC. Nearly every single major national scientific body around the world unreservedly supports the work and findings of the IPCC.

Did you hear what I just said? Is my English OK? Is the microphone on? Because I'm beginning to wonder.

During the last six months I have travelled around Europe for hundreds of hours in trains, electric cars and buses, repeating these life-changing words over and over again. But no one seems to be talking about it, and nothing has changed. In fact, the emissions are still rising.

When I have been travelling around to speak in different countries, I am always offered help to write about the specific climate policies in specific countries. But that is not really necessary. Because the basic problem is the same everywhere. And the basic problem is that basically nothing is being done to halt – or even slow – climate and ecological breakdown, despite all the beautiful words and promises.

The UK is, however, very special. Not only for its mind-blowing historical carbon debt, but also for its current, very creative, carbon accounting.

Since 1990 the UK has achieved a 37% reduction of its territorial CO_2 emissions, according to the Global Carbon Project. And that does sound very impressive. But these numbers do not include emissions from aviation, shipping and those associated with imports and exports. If these numbers are included the reduction is around 10% since 1990, or an average of 0.4% a year, according to Tyndall Manchester.

And the main reason for this reduction is not a consequence of climate policies, but rather a 2001 EU directive on air quality that essentially forced the UK to close down its very old and extremely dirty coal power plants and replace them with less dirty gas power stations. And switching from one disastrous energy source to a slightly less disastrous one will of course result in a lowering of emissions.

But perhaps the most dangerous misconception about the climate crisis is that we have to 'lower' our emissions. Because that is far from enough. Our emissions have to stop if we are to stay below 1.5–2°C of warming. The 'lowering of emissions' is of course necessary, but it is only the beginning of a fast process that must lead to a stop within a couple of decades, or less. And by 'stop' I mean net zero – and then quickly on to negative figures. That rules out most of today's politics.

The fact that we are speaking of 'lowering' instead of 'stopping' emissions is perhaps the greatest force behind the continuing business as usual. The UK's active current support of new exploitation of fossil fuels – for example, the UK shale gas fracking industry, the expansion of its North Sea oil and gas fields, the expansion of airports as well as the planning permission for a brand new coal mine – is beyond absurd.

This ongoing irresponsible behaviour will no doubt be remembered in history as one of the greatest failures of humankind.

The climate crisis is both the easiest and the hardest issue we have ever faced. The easiest because we know what we must do. We must stop the emissions of greenhouse gases. The hardest because our current economics are still totally dependent on burning fossil fuels, and thereby destroying ecosystems in order to create everlasting economic growth.

'So, exactly how do we solve that?' you ask us, the schoolchildren striking for the climate.

And we say: 'No one knows for sure. But we have to stop burning fossil fuels and restore nature and many other things that we may not have quite figured out yet.'

Then you say: 'That's not an answer!'

So we say: 'We have to start treating the crisis like a crisis – and act even if we don't have all the solutions.'

'That's still not an answer,' you say.

Then we start talking about circular economy and rewilding nature and the need for a just transition. Then you don't understand what we are talking about.

We say that all those solutions needed are not known to anyone and therefore we must unite behind the science and find them together along the way. But you do not listen to that. Because those answers are for solving a crisis that most of you don't even fully understand. Or don't want to understand.

You don't listen to the science because you are only interested in solutions that will enable you to carry on like before. Like now. And those answers don't exist any more. Because you did not act in time.

Avoiding climate breakdown will require cathedral thinking. We must lay the foundation while we may not know exactly how to build the ceiling.

Sometimes we just simply have to find a way. The moment we decide to fulfil something, we can do anything. And I'm sure that the moment we start behaving as if we were in an emergency, we can avoid climate and ecological catastrophe. Humans are very adaptable: we can still fix this. But the opportunity to do so will not last for long. We must start today. We have no more excuses.

We children are not sacrificing our education and our childhood for you to tell us what you consider is politically possible in the society that you have created. We have not taken to the streets for you to take selfies with us and tell us that you really admire what we do.

We children are doing this to wake the adults up. We children are doing this for you to put your differences aside and start acting as you would in a crisis. We children are doing this because we want our hopes and dreams back.

I hope my microphone was on. I hope you could all hear me.

DAME ANITA RODDICK

(1942–2007)

MORALITY IS NOT A LUXURY

Having lived just outside Littlehampton as a kid, I got one of my first jobs in the Body Shop factory. It had inspirational quotes all over the walls, Brownies would come on factory tours to see how bath bombs were made, and it smelt like White Musk.

Roddick was a national treasure. Think Deborah Meaden meets Greta Thunberg. She fought for fair trade, the environment and animal rights. She was a firebrand of ethical consumerism. And she was our most famous woman entrepreneur.

Speaking to the International Forum on globalisation in 1999, she painted a picture of a global market that benefited from insecurity and worked for elites. She then challenged the audience to try living in a world without morality, if they thought 'morality is a luxury business can't afford'. This was a huge vision – business had to change. Two decades later, we have to ask the question: has it?

We can ask the same question of the gleaming towers of Wall Street or the City of London – and the powerful men and women who tinker with the money system which drives world trade. Who is this system for?

Let's look more closely. Every day, the gleaming towers of high finance oversee a global flow of two trillion dollars through their computer screens. And the terrifying thing is that only 3% of that – that's three hundredths – has anything to do with trade at all. Let alone free trade between equal communities.

It has everything to do with money. The great global myth being that the current world trade system is for anything but money.

The other 97% of the two trillion is speculation. It is froth – but froth with terrifying power over people's lives. Reducing powerless communities, access to basic human rights can make money, but not for them. But then the system isn't designed for them.

It isn't designed for you and me either. We, all of us, rich and poor, have to live with the insecurity caused by an out of control global casino with a built-in bias towards instability. Because it is instability that makes money for the money-traders.

'The great enemy of the truth is very often not the lie – deliberate, contrived and dishonest,' said John F Kennedy, 'but the myth – persistent, persuasive and unrealistic.' Asking questions can puncture these powerful myths.

I spend much of every year travelling around the world, talking to people in the front line of globalisation: women, community farmers, children. I know how unrealistic these myths are. Not just in developing countries, but right under our noses.

Like the small farmers of the US, 500 of which go out of business every week.

Half a century ago there were a million black farmers in the US. Now there are 1,800. Globalisation means that the subsidies go to the big farms, while the small family farms – the heart of so many American communities – go to the wall.

Or the dark, cramped factories where people work for a pittance for 12-hour days without a day off. 'The workers are not allowed to talk to each other and they didn't allow us to go to the bathroom,' says one Asian worker in that garment factory. Not in Seoul. Not in São Paulo. But in San Francisco.

We have a world trading system that is blind to this kind of injustice. And as the powers of governments shrink, this system is, in effect, our new unelected, uncontrollable world government. One that outlaws our attempts to make things better.

According to the WTO, we don't have the right to discriminate between tuna caught without killing dolphins and tuna caught by those who don't care, don't worry and don't try.

According to the WTO, we have no right to hoard patented seeds from one harvest to plant the following year.

According to the WTO, we have no right to discriminate against beef with growth hormones.

According to the WTO, the livelihoods of the small-scale banana farmers of the Windward Islands are worthless – now facing ruin as the WTO favours the big US exporters.

The truth is that the WTO, and the group of unelected trade officials who run it, are now the world's highest court, with the right to overturn local laws and safety regulations wherever they say it 'interferes with trade'.

This is world government by default, but it is a blind government. It looks at the measurements of money, but it can't see anything else. It can recognise profits and losses, but it deliberately turns its face away from human rights, child labour or keeping the environment viable for future generations.

It is government without heart, and without heart you find the creativity of the human spirit starts to dwindle too.

Now there will be commentators and politicians by the truckload over the next week accusing us of wanting to turn the clock back. They will say we are parochial, inward-looking, xenophobic and dangerous.

But we must remind them what free trade really is. The truth is that 'free trade' was originally about the freedom of communities to trade equally with each other.

It was never intended to be what it is today. A licence for the big, the powerful and the rich to ride roughshod over the small, the weak and the poor.

And while we're about it, let's nail another myth.

Nobody could be more in favour of a global outlook than I am. Internationalism means that we can see into the dark corners of the world and hold those companies to account when they are devastating forests or employing children as bonded labour. Globalisation is the complete opposite. Its rules pit country against country and workers against workers in the blinkered pursuit of international competitiveness.

Internationalism means we can link together at local level across the world and use our power as consumers. Working together, across all sectors, we can turn businesses from private greed to public good. It means, even more importantly, that we can start understanding each other in a way that no generation has managed before. Let's be clear about this. It's not trade we're against, it's exploitation and unchecked power.

I don't pretend for a moment that we're perfect at The Body Shop. Or that every one of our experiments works out – especially when it comes to building trading relationships that actually strengthen poor communities.

We are absolutely committed to increasing our trade with communities around the world, because this is the key – not just for our future, but the planet's. It means that they trade to strengthen their local economy for profit, but not because their very survival depends on it.

Community trade will make us not a multinational, but a multi-local. I hope we can measure our success in terms of our ability to show just what's possible if a company genuinely opens a dialogue with communities.

Heaven knows, we're not there yet. But this is real life, and all any of us can do is to make sure we are going in the right direction and never lose our determination to improve. The trouble is that the current trading system undermines anybody who tries.

Businesses which forego profits to build communities, or keep production local rather than employing semi-slaves in distant sweatshops, risk losing business to cheaper competitors without such commitments, and being targeted for takeover by the slash-and-burn corporate raiders reinforced by the weight of the WTO.

It's difficult for all of us. But if we are going to change the world then nobody – not governments, not the media, not individuals – is going to get a free ride. And certainly not business, because business is now faster, more creative and far wealthier than governments ever were.

Business has to be a force for social change. It is not enough to avoid hideous evil – it must, we must, actively do good. If business stays parochial, without moral energy or codes of behaviour, claiming there are no such thing as values, then God help us all. If you think morality is a luxury business can't afford, try living in a world without it.

So what should we do at this critical moment in world history? First, we must make sure this week that we lay the foundations for humanising world trade.

We must learn from our experience of what really works for poor countries, poor communities around the world. The negotiators this week must listen to these communities and allow these countries full participation and contribution to trade negotiations.

The rules have got to change. We need a radical alternative that puts people before profit. And that brings us to my second prescription. We must start measuring our success differently. If politicians, businesses and analysts only measure the bottom line – the growth in money – then it's not surprising the world is skewed. It's not surprising that the WTO is half-blind, recognising slash-and-burn corporations but not the people they destroy.

It's not surprising that it values flipping hamburgers or making sweaters at 50 cents an hour as a valuable activity, but takes no account of those other jobs – the caring, educating and loving work that we all know needs doing if we're going to turn the world into a place we want to live.

Let's measure the success of places and corporations against how much they enhance human well-being. Body Shop was one of the first companies to submit itself to a social audit, and many others are now doing so. Measuring what really matters can give us the revolution in kindness we so desperately need. That's the real bottom line.

And finally, we must remember we already have power as consumers and as organisations forming strategic and increasingly influential alliances for change. They can insist on open markets as much as they like, but if consumers won't buy, nothing on earth can make them. Just look at how European consumers have forced the biotech industry's back up against the wall.

We have to be political consumers, vigilante consumers. With the barrage of propaganda served up to us every day, we have to be. We must be wise enough so that, whatever they may decide at the trade talks, we know where to put our energy and our money. No matter what we're told or cajoled to do, we must work together to get the truth out in co-operation for the best, not competition for the cheapest.

By putting our money where our heart is, refusing to buy the products which exploit, by forming powerful strategic alliances, we will mould the world into a kinder, more loving shape. And we will do so no matter what you decide this week.

Human progress is on our side.

BARONESS BERTHA VON SUTTNER
(1843-1914)
NOBEL LECTURE ON THE PEACE MOVEMENT

Von Suttner was born into the aristocracy of the Austrian court, but ran away with her husband to the Caucasus, when his family disapproved of the union. There she wrote and read, and went from militaristic aristocrat to philosophic, pacifist poet and novelist. And later, the second woman to become a Nobel laureate and first to be awarded the Nobel Peace Prize.

In 1889 she published *Die Waffen nieder!* (*Lay Down Your Arms*), an anti-war book about the traumatising effects of war. Its impact made her a leader in the peace movement. Here is her Nobel Lecture on that Peace Movement, delivered in 1906.

One of the eternal truths is that happiness is created and developed in peace, and one of the eternal rights is the individual's right to live. The strongest of all instincts, that of self-preservation, is an assertion of this right, affirmed and sanctified by the ancient commandment 'Thou shalt not kill'.

It is unnecessary for me to point out how little this right and this commandment are respected in the present state of civilisation. Up to the present time, the military organisation of our society has been founded upon a denial of the possibility of peace, a contempt for the value of human life and an acceptance of the urge to kill.

And because this has been so, as far back as world history records (and how short is the actual time, for what are a few thousand years?), most people believe that it must always remain so. That the world is ever-changing and developing is still not generally recognised, since the knowledge of the laws of evolution, which control all life, whether in the geological timespan or in society, belongs to a recent period of scientific development.

It is erroneous to believe that the future will of necessity continue the trends of the past and the present. The past and present move away from us in the stream of time like the passing landscape of the riverbanks, as the vessel carrying mankind is borne inexorably by the current towards new shores.

That the future will always be one degree better than what is past and discarded is the conviction of those who understand the laws of evolution and try to assist their action. Only through the understanding and deliberate application of natural laws and forces, in the material domain as well as in the moral, will the technical devices and the social institutions be created which will make our lives easier, richer and more noble. These things are called ideals as long as they exist in the realm of ideas; they stand as achievements of progress as soon as they are transformed into visible, living and effective forms.

'If you keep me in touch with developments, and if I hear that the Peace Movement is moving along the road of practical activity, then I will help it on with money.'

These words were spoken by that eminent Scandinavian to whom I owe this opportunity of appearing before you today, Ladies and Gentlemen. Alfred Nobel said them when my husband and I visited with him in 1892 in Bern, where a peace congress was in progress.

His will showed that he had gradually become convinced that the movement had emerged from the fog of pious theories into the light of attainable and realistically envisaged goals. He recognised science and idealistic literature as pursuits which foster culture and help civilisation. With these goals he ranked the objectives of the peace congresses: the attainment of international justice and the consequent reduction in the size of armies.

Once a new system begins to emerge, the old ones must fall. The conviction that it is possible, that is necessary and that it would be a blessing to have an assured judicial peace between nations is already deeply embedded in all social strata, even in those that wield the power. The task is already so clearly outlined, and so many are already working on it, that it must sooner or later be accomplished. A few years ago there was not a single minister of state professing the ideals of the peace movement. Today there are already many heads of state who do so.

Let us look round us in the world of today and see whether we are really justified in claiming for pacifism progressive development and positive results. A terrible war, unprecedented in the world's history, recently raged in the Far East. This war was followed by a revolution, even more terrible, which shook the giant Russian empire, a revolution whose final outcome we cannot yet foresee. We hear continually of fire, robbery, bombings, executions, overflowing prisons, beatings and massacres; in short, an orgy of the Demon Violence.

Meanwhile, in Central and Western Europe, which narrowly escaped war, we have distrust, threats, sabre rattling, press baiting, feverish naval build up, and rearming everywhere. In England, Germany and France, novels are appearing in which the plot of a future surprise attack by a neighbour is intended as a spur to even more fervent arming. Fortresses are being erected, submarines built, whole areas mined, airships tested for use in war; and all this with such zeal – as if to attack one's neighbour were the most inevitable and important function of a state. Even the printed programme of the second Hague Conference [to be held in 1907] proclaims it as virtually a council of war. Now in the face of all this, can people still maintain that the peace movement is making progress?

Well, we must not be blinded by the obvious; we must also look for the new growth pushing up from the ground below. We must understand that two philosophies, two eras of civilisation, are wrestling with one another and that a vigorous new spirit is supplanting the blatant and threatening old. No longer weak and formless, this promising new life is already widely established and determined to survive. Quite apart from the peace movement, which is a symptom rather than a cause of actual change, there is taking place in the world a process of internationalisation and unification. Factors contributing to the development of this process are technical inventions, improved communications, economic interdependence and closer international relations. The instinct of self-preservation in human society, acting almost subconsciously, as do all drives in the human mind, is rebelling against the constantly refined methods of annihilation and against the destruction of humanity.

When [Theodore] Roosevelt received me in the White House on October 17th 1904, he said to me, 'World peace is coming, it certainly is coming, but only step by step.'

And so it is. However clearly envisaged, however apparently near and within reach the goal may be, the road to it must be traversed a step at a time, and countless obstacles surmounted on the way.

Furthermore, we are dealing with a goal as yet not perceived by many millions or, if perceived, regarded as a utopian dream. Also, powerful vested interests are involved, interests trying to maintain the old order and to prevent the goal's being reached. The adherents of the old order have a powerful ally in the natural law of inertia inherent in humanity which is, as it were, a natural defence against change. Thus pacifism faces no easy struggle.

This question of whether violence or law shall prevail between states is the most vital of the problems of our eventful era, and the most serious in its repercussions. The beneficial results of a secure world peace are almost inconceivable, but even more inconceivable are the consequences of the threatening world war which many misguided people are prepared to precipitate. The advocates of pacifism are well aware how meagre are their resources of personal influence and power. They know that they are still few in number and weak in authority, but when they realistically consider themselves and the ideal they serve, they see themselves as the servants of the greatest of all causes. On the solution of this problem depends whether our Europe will become a showpiece of ruins and failure, or whether we can avoid this danger and so enter sooner the coming era of secure peace and law in which a civilisation of unimagined glory will develop.

The many aspects of this question are what the second Hague Conference should be discussing rather than the proposed topics concerning the laws and practices of war at sea, the bombardment of ports, towns and villages, the laying of mines and so on. The contents of this agenda demonstrate that,

although the supporters of the existing structure of society, which accepts war, come to a peace conference prepared to modify the nature of war, they are basically trying to keep the present system intact.

The advocates of pacifism, inside and outside the Conference, will, however, defend their objectives and press forward another step towards their goal – the goal which, to repeat Roosevelt's words, affirms the duty of his government and of all governments 'to bring nearer the time when the sword shall not be the arbiter among nations'.

VIVIENNE MING

(1971–)

THE FUTURE OF HUMAN POTENTIAL

Ming is a world-renowned theoretical neuroscientist and artificial intelligence expert. One of the BBC 100 Women in 2017, she is recognised as an LGBT leader and is outspoken about her experiences with mental health issues.

In this incredible, visionary talk, given at SingularityU in South Africa in 2017, she shares a vision of how technology can augment human potential, and answers the question: how do we make sure artificial intelligence makes us better?

OK. I can pretty much predict what some of the questions will be later during the panel. Do you agree with Elon or Mark? Which of our jobs are gonna get taken away? I'm actually genuinely happy to answer all of those – the general tenor of my answer is it's all a bunch of bullshit.

That doesn't mean that artificial intelligence and machine learning is bullshit. In fact it's profound and it will have a profound impact on us as a society, on our economic potential. And in human potential. And that's my real interest point. This is nominally a talk about AI, but really it's going to be a talk about people. Because in the end technology is just a tool. It doesn't magically make anything better or worse. It's the choices we make. It's what we decide to do with it that really matters. Some of the choices we've made to date haven't been the best.

But we've got a lot of time to change that direction. Now tomorrow there's gonna be a panel on the future of work and unfortunately I have to fly back to California tonight. And so I won't be here. I would have loved to have helped on that panel so I'm going to try and set it up for them by saying something a little provocative. Human capital is a toxic asset. I don't know how much a given human's going to be worth 20 years from now but I virtually guarantee you if we don't change the way we build people, they will be worth vastly less than we think they are. And that will have a profound and disruptive impact on our society.

So these are some illustrations. I was once asked to write a little Op Ed about the future of work and in the spirit of just sort of being a jerk, I instead wrote a short story about a young man, a financial analyst who had done everything right.

He went to college, he got good grades, he worked hard, he got the right job at a great company and it was his last day of work because a deep reinforcement network that he and his co-workers had unknowingly trained up just by doing their own job was taking their jobs from them.

The career paths that will be the most profoundly disrupted within, let's say the next five to ten years, it is, generically speaking, professional services. Financial advising, legal, basic doctors. If you know what you're going to advise your clients before they walk in the door, I'm going to build an AI that's gonna do it better, faster, cheaper than you.

But that isn't what this story has to be about, so when I talk about AI, I don't talk about how to target ads better. I don't talk about how to optimise supply chains. Those are absolutely things that this sort of work can do. But I'm going to talk about human potential and the reason why AI is such an amazing thing and how it truly can improve the world.

. . .

Gallup estimates that there are about 130 million people that are actively engaged in their work worldwide. A rounding error in the global population. We had a pretty good slice of that group. And I got to build models that predicted how good you were at jobs that you had never held. Our goal was kind of ambitious: take bias out of the hiring process. Broadly defined, race and gender, absolutely, but did you really need to go to MIT to do this job? Is someone that worked at Google better than someone that didn't have a brand name company on their résumé?

So, what we found was what wasn't predictive of long-term outcomes: grades, test scores. The university you went to, at least once I knew other things about you. Even the skill sets. We define our hiring and our education system on skills. There is no skill which is robot-proof. Period. Nothing. No skill or knowledge. Someone like me can build a tool to do it better, faster and cheaper.

Why do we persist in building humans to do the samething that machines can do better? When there's a fundamental truth which is much more exciting.

Which is we actually know just what people can do to be robot-proof, and in one of our earlier speakers you saw a list of the social and cognitive qualities that we know are predictive of life outcomes.

As those qualities increase in the population, people live longer. They're happier, they're more socially connected, they have increased income, greater total wealth. And even in measures of things like subjective happiness or congenital measures of health outcomes. How you think affects how your body expresses congenital defects. That's amazing. And it has nothing to do with how we build and educate people today.

That is profoundly disappointing, but it doesn't need to be. So we built this thing and it predicted grades and grades don't predict shit. OK. What if we can take a similarly amazing AI. Let's say it's gonna analyse the speech patterns of young kids and another AI which can analyse the artwork of my daughter.

She draws so many pictures that I think there are whole forests in Brazil that don't exist any more just because of her mania for drawing. It all goes right into the compost. What if you just take a picture of it and a deep neural network analyses those speech patterns, maybe asks questions of parents and from that makes the most insane predictions you can imagine? How long will this child live? How happy will they be? How far will they go in their education and how much of an impact will they have on the world?

So it turns out the worst thing you could do is actually make such a prediction and then tell the parents. The cursed crystal ball; it only makes things worse. We know this, actually. Measuring people and treating them as fixed quantities, just profiling them, doesn't make the world a better place. But we built AIs to do exactly that. And in a project we call Muse, what it does instead of telling their parents, 'Hey! Your kid's going to win a Nobel Prize, yours is gonna flunk out.' Every single night, purely via estimates, it sends them a simple 20-minute activity, a game to play with their kids, a game specifically designed for that child to maximise their life outcomes.

Again, this is what AI can do. This is how AI can make better people. So let's.

. . .

So this is my challenge to you to end on. Do you feel better after you've spent an hour on Facebook? Do you feel like your phone, not when you're using it, but after you've set it down, has made you a better person? This is my challenge myself. For me it's a hard rule – technology must always challenge us.

You have to be a better person than when you had it on in the first place. And if it's not achieving that, we are robbing from our own future. This is my goal for AI: how do we make certain AI only makes us better? Always make certain it's challenging us? The goal of all of these systems, the goal of the education, of the health, of restructuring the way we run our companies, should be explicitly about making better people. That's what augmented intelligence can be.

MARY WOLLSTONECRAFT

(1759–1797)

UTOPIAN DREAMS

Wollstonecraft is considered THE prototype feminist. She was born into a struggling family, with an abusive father, in Spitalfields, east London, a stone's throw away from where I am writing this book now.

Having wanted the kind of education her brother was given, she was determined women should be educated, and opened a school for girls by age 25, though they struggled to make it work. She tried her hand at being a governess, but it was the radical publisher Joseph Johnson who gave her the break, publishing her first book, *Thoughts on the Education of Daughters*.

Wollstonecraft attracted the company of the radical thinkers of her time, and it wasn't long before she published *A Vindication of the Rights of Woman* – considered a feminist masterpiece. It contains this passage, one I'm reimagining as a speech, which isn't too much of a leap, for she would have engaged in dinner table debate with her radical friends. In it she makes the visionary proclamation of a utopian dream – one where women are as free as men.

These may be termed utopian dreams. Thanks to that Being who impressed them on my soul, and gave me sufficient strength of mind to dare to exert my own reason, till, becoming dependent only on him for the support of my virtue,

I view with indignation the mistaken notions that enslave my sex.

I love man as my fellow; but his sceptre, real or usurped, extends not to me, unless the reason of an individual demands my homage; and even then the submission is to reason, and not to man. In fact, the conduct of an accountable being must be regulated by the operations of its own reason; or on what foundation rests the throne of God?

It appears to me necessary to dwell on these obvious truths, because females have been insulated, as it were; and, while they have been stripped of the virtues that should clothe humanity, they have been decked with artificial graces that enable them to exercise a short-lived tyranny.

Love, in their bosoms, taking place of every nobler passion, their sole ambition is to be fair, to raise emotion instead of inspiring respect; and this ignoble desire, like the servility in absolute monarchies, destroys all strength of character. Liberty is the mother of virtue, and if women be, by their very constitution, slaves, and not allowed to breathe the sharp, invigorating air of freedom, they must ever languish like exotics, and be reckoned beautiful flaws in nature.

HOW TO BE
OUTSPOKEN ...

My phone wallpaper is an Oprah quote. (See Chapter 1 for why that's no surprise.) It says: 'You get in life what you have the courage to ask for.' Which is kinda similar to what my Spanish friend, Gloria, tells me is a famous Spanish saying; roughly translated it goes something like: 'The crying baby gets fed.' Now, I'm not one for inspirational Instagram memes, but I can get on board with both of these, because I'm not sure there's anything more fundamental than speaking out.

We have one life. If we want to achieve something, change something, build something, be given an opportunity, be understood – we are going to have to say it!

This isn't about being a Diva, you don't need puppies in your dressing room. Hang on! I DO need puppies in my dressing room! But, in all seriousness, this is about being heard and giving yourself the best chance in life.

So for those of us who were taught it was rude to ask for what you want, we are going to have to practise being outspoken. We're going to have to try that everyday free speech, saying yes to things we agree with, and saying no to things we don't, and build from there.

And where do you build to? Well, there are many different types of speeches, but when I spoke to Dr Susan Jones, speechwriter to Prime Ministers, she explained that there were three main types. They are to do with:

- The past. These are forensic: 'I'd like to present to you a lecture on the history of jam.'
- The present. These are ceremonial: 'Here's to my best friend, the Bride, thank you for making me Maid of Honour. I'm sorry I drank all the Prosecco (hiccup).'
- And the future. These are political: 'Brexit means Brexit.'

When writing a speech, start with something everyone can agree on: 'We all like cheese.' Set up a complication. 'But the dairy industry can be cruel.' Offer the solution: 'Buy vegan cheese, everyone!'

Now, the biggest problem with being outspoken, and what puts a lot of us off, is that you will come across conflict. People will disagree with you. Dairy cheese manufacturers perhaps! But let's take comfort in the fact that ALL the women in this book have been called disagreeable by someone. Some will even be disliked by millions of people.

Not only will people argue, people will tell you you're doing it wrong. Pedants will tell you your grammar isn't acceptable, or it's crass to use the word 'kinda'. But you don't have to be perfect to have your say. And it's OK if someone disagrees with the content of what you have to say. We can handle that. The other person might be right, we might all learn something.

Take a breath, take your space, say your piece and let's all remember to listen to others too. To be friends with people who think differently from us, to surround ourselves with women as diverse as the women in this book.

I hope you have found new friendly voices in this book, and become reacquainted with familiar ones. Women who inspire you. Google them, ask for their books for Christmas and write their soundbites somewhere special for when you need them most. Take screenshots and make your phone wallpaper something you NEED to remember.

Acknowledgements

THANK YOUS

All the women who agreed to be in this book – thank you so much for trusting me with your words.

Yvonne Jacob, Victoria Hall, Juliet Pickering, Hattie Grunewald – thank you for making this book happen. Can we go for a wine now please?

Thanks to the people who helped make *Yap Yap Yap* (the show that inspired this book) happen in the first place … Gaggle, Fig 2, Outset, WOW Festival, Troublemakers Festival, Dr Anne Karpf, Holly Aylett, Dr Susan Jones, Fatoş Usek, Domino Pateman, Jade Coles, Georgina Bednar, Jamie Rose Monk, Ama Josephine Eclair, Charlotte Church, Ruth Barnes, Paula Varjack, Dana Jade, Georgia Griffiths, Sally George, Helen Keeley, Alison Lenihan, Bethan James, Su Pollard, Shazia Mirza, Nicola Coughlan.

Thanks to Kate for sharing salads with me at the British Library.

Thanks to Emily for taking the strain at Studio X and getting good snacks.

Thanks to the Coughlins and the Bricknalls for your support.

And the biggest thanks to Steve for being the kind of man who buys *Everyday Sexism* and makes me dinners. Love you.

Credits

Oprah Winfrey: Speech courtesy of Harpo Inc.

Audre Lorde: Speech courtesy of Audre Lorde.

Mashish Alinejad: Speech courtesy of Mashih Alinejad, author of the 2018 memoir *The Wind in My Hair*.

Margaret Sanger: Speech courtesy of the estate of Margaret Sanger.

Sarah Weddington: Speech courtesy of Sarah Weddington on behalf of Jane Roe.

Annie Sprinkle: Speech courtesy of Annie Sprinkle.

Kelli Jean Drinkwater: Speech courtesy of Kelli Jean Drinkwater.

Michelle Obama: Speech courtesy of Michelle Obama Manchester, New Hampshire Speech in 2007.

Beverley (Bev) Palesa Ditsie: Speech courtesy of Bev Palesa Ditsie - Drafted by The Beijing '95 Lesbian Caucus, including Bev Palesa Ditsie, Rachel Rosenbloom, Gloria Careaga, Rebeca Sevilla, Julie Dorf and Nicky Mcintyre.

Rose's Speech from *Fences*: courtesy of the estate of August Wilson.

Nora Ephron: Speech courtesy of the estate of Nora Ephron.

Charlotte Church: Speech courtesy of Charlotte Church.

Greta Thunberg: Speech courtesy of Greta Thunberg.

Dame Anita Roddick: Speech courtesy of the estate of Dame Anita Roddick (1942 To 2007), Founder of The Body Shop.

Vivienne Ming: Speech courtesy of Dr Vivienne Ming.